Judging Judges

Simon Lee was educated at Oxford and Yale. He is Professor of Jurisprudence at The Queen's University of Belfast and the author of the widely acclaimed *Law and Morals* (1986). He judges judges regularly in the legal journals, the press and on radio and television.

D1638395

Judging Judges

———

Simon Lee

faber and faber
LONDON · BOSTON

First published in 1988
by Faber and Faber Limited
3 Queen Square London WC1N 3AU
Reprinted 1988
This paperback edition first published
with an additional chapter in 1989

Photoset by Wilmaset Birkenhead Wirral
Printed in Great Britain by
Richard Clay Ltd, Bungay, Suffolk
All rights reserved

British Library Cataloguing in Publication Data

Lee. Simon
Judging judges.
1. England. Judiciary. Role
I. Title
344.207′14
ISBN 0-571-14139-0

For Patricia,
Jamie, Katie and Rebecca
with love and thanks

Contents

———

Contents

Preface to the paperback edition

———

I was delighted by four immediate reactions to the hardback edition of this book. First, the people for whom it was intended seemed to find it helpful or at least thought-provoking. Second, the book sold out within a couple of days of publication and had to be reprinted. Third, it annoyed all the right people. Fourth, the publishers suggested a paperback edition to reach a wider range of students and other potential readers. They also kindly offered me extra space to reply to some of those who were outraged by the initial version of the book. I was tempted to rebut detailed criticisms one by one, in the grand manner of Professor Dworkin's replies to critics. On reflection, however, I thought it would be more interesting for the reader to imagine how the book was received in the heartland of its critics, hence the new last chapter, 'Judging Judges on Appeal'. I have also taken advantage of this opportunity to make a few corrections but otherwise I have resisted the temptation to update, for instance, the main text of the *Spycatcher* chapter. That must await a second edition. Nevertheless, it is appropriate to record that the Law Lords' final 1988 judgment in the *Spycatcher* case fulfilled the expectations of that chapter.

Preface

———

1987 was a vintage year for judging judges. It was the year when the British press attacked the judges time and again, most spectacularly when the newspapers themselves lost the first rounds of the *Spycatcher* case. It was the year when the American public celebrated the bicentenary of its Constitution with the acrimonious battle to defeat Judge Bork's nomination to the Supreme Court. It was also the Year of the Three Lord Chancellors with Lords Hailsham, Havers and Mackay following one another in quick succession as the head of the British judiciary. This book seeks to make sense of these events and of some other celebrated cases and judges of the 1980s in order to prepare us for judging judges in the 1990s and beyond.

So how do judges decide hard cases? How should they? At least three groups need to think of answers to these questions. First, law students will need to develop responses in order to understand their subject. Second, followers of current affairs, and indeed the media who lead current affairs, increasingly find the courts involved in matters of moral and political import and so will need to form opinions on the proper scope of judicial power. A third group of potential readers is, I hope, the judges themselves and those who appear before them or seek to change their minds, all of whom must formulate some vision of the judicial role.

This book seeks to help those three kinds of readers. It identifies the most common misconceptions about judicial law-making, suggests a better analysis, explores famous cases of the last decade to illustrate these points, then looks at famous judges of that period to see whether they had developed answers themselves, examines suggestions for reform, considers the American experience and finally draws some tentative conclusions.

This is not an elitist book which is designed to be read solely by members of the jurisprudential jet-set. It is instead a development of my teaching and my writing in legal journals and the press. I am grateful for the stimulus which students and editors have provided. I owe much to Will Sulkin, who guided my book on *Law and Morals* through Oxford University Press and who is now a director of the marvellously patient Faber and Faber.

Many members of my family, friends, teachers, students and colleagues have helped shape my thoughts. In particular, I would like to thank John Bell, Guido Calabresi, Sandra Fredman, Ian Kennedy, Christoper McCrudden, Joseph Raz and Simon Whittaker. But none has seen this text and most would recoil in horror from some of my views.

Patricia, my wife, and Jamie, Katie and Rebecca, our children, deserve most appreciation. Patricia not only bought the word-processor on which I have tapped out this text, but also she and the children tolerated the hours I spent with it. I am delighted to have something to show for these efforts and to be able again to dedicate a book to my family with love and thanks.

Part I

Theories

——

Fairy Tales, Noble Dreams and Nightmares

Fairy tales, noble dreams and nightmares have long bedevilled attempts to judge judges. Whether they are striking down Ken Livingstone's GLC scheme to reduce fares on London Transport, upholding the Prime Minister's ban on trade unions at GCHQ, rejecting Victoria Gillick's challenge to the legality of teenage contraception without parental consent, deciding against Arthur Scargill's striking miners, authorizing the sterilization of a mentally handicapped teenager without her consent, or banning Peter Wright's book, *Spycatcher*, judges have the opportunity to make law. That function is of such fundamental importance to our democracy that judges can, and should, expect informed criticism. Retired Law Lords trundle on to television and radio to say how they would have decided differently. Academics flit across the television screen trying to explain what happened. But all too often the judges' critics fail to construct an appropriate framework within which to judge judges. They fall prey to the fairy tales, dreams and nightmares.

The fairy tale was exposed by Lord Reid, the leading Law Lord of the 1960s and early 1970s:

> Those with a taste for fairy tales seem to have thought that in some Aladdin's cave there is hidden the Common Law in all its splendour and that on a judge's appointment there descends on him knowledge of the magic words Open Sesame. Bad decisions are given when the judge has muddled the password and the wrong door opens. But we do not believe in fairy tales any more.

The most sophisticated embellishment of this fairy tale has been described as a Noble Dream. That was Professor Hart's assessment of Professor Dworkin's theory of adjudication. Dworkin argues that there is always one single right answer embedded in the principles which underlie the law. This seems implausible but Dworkin has developed his argument so as to emphasize that Aladdin's role is more creative than merely incanting Open Sesame. There are indications that some British judges are beginning to take Dworkin's rights thesis seriously. In particular, he has argued that judges should concentrate on principles and ignore policy arguments and some judges have begun to adopt that rhetoric. But Dworkin's approach makes more sense in his and its native setting of the United States of America. Unlike its creator, who is simultaneously Professor of Jurisprudence at Oxford and Professor of Law at New York University, his theory does not cross the Atlantic very easily.

More cynical observers of judicial decision-making do not believe in fairy tales, nor do they indulge in Noble Dreaming. Instead they suffer, according to Hart once again, from Nightmares. Their nightmare is that judges have complete freedom to make the law as they think fit. A British variation on this approach goes further to say that the judges use their discretion to further their own class interest in the name of the public interest. Professor John Griffith of the London School of Economics (LSE) is the most famous academic to imagine this recurring nightmare.

All three fantasies come from within the legal community. Can we turn outside for enlightenment on how to judge judges? Politicians, for example, often purport to judge judges. Cynics would say that the propensity with which MPs will rush to criticize the latest decision rises as their majority decreases and thus their need for publicity increases. But one does not have to be that cynical to conclude that the same old tired nonsense emerges from politicians as from lawyers on this topic of judging judges. The standard television panel of MPs in the immediate aftermath of a controversial decision produces the same fantasies.

Conservative MPs favour the fairy tale. One or another can usually be found to defend the judges by saying that they are simply applying the law. This is palpable nonsense, as a moment's thought about, say, the Gillick case will show. How can it be so simple when there is a 3–2 split in the House of Lords, overturning a 0–3 decision in the Court of Appeal which was itself overturning the High Court?

A Social or Liberal Democrat MP, if one can be found at all, can be guaranteed to articulate the thrust of the Noble Dream by waffling on about the underlying liberal principles of the law, claiming that the case shows that the judges cannot be trusted to protect our civil liberties and that we therefore need a Bill of Rights. The logic here is again difficult to follow. The conclusion, the call for a Bill of Rights, gives more power to the very people the premise says we cannot trust, the judges who will interpret the vague document.

A Labour MP will allege that the decision reflects the judges' class bias – what else could one expect from a white, male, old, rich, upper-middle-class, public-school and Oxbridge type? The adjectives are meant to refer to the judge, not the Labour MP, but the need to point that out shows in itself that this line of attack is unduly simplistic. The most privileged of people, such as Tony Benn, can be the most radical of thinkers.

All this suggests that we are being told more about the commentators than those they are meant to be commentating upon, we learn more about the prejudices of the critics than about those of the judges. This is not necessarily unhealthy, it may even be inevitable, but it does need to be recognized. Both Griffith and Dworkin, for example, seem to be saying little more than that they would have reached different results from the ones they criticize. This is the case with many jurisprudential problems. As an expression at Yale Law School in the 1970s would put it, Griffith and Dworkin are each presenting 'one view of the cathedral'. The allusion is to Monet's studies of the cathedral at Rouen. The great Impressionist painted the cathedral in different lights. No single picture is 'right'. Each adds to our understanding of the cathedral. If I can develop the story and imagine that various painters are portraying the cathedral from all angles, then it will become apparent that each picture adds something to our appreciation both of the cathedral and of the artist. In particular, we can tell whether the artist is painting the cathedral of law from a left- or right-wing perspective. Griffith and Dworkin tell us more about themselves, perhaps, than about the judges but they do give us some insight into the judicial process which needs to be preserved. Neither, however, offers a well-rounded portrait.

The failure of analysis hitherto has left the whole process of judicial law-making shrouded in obscurity. Of course, some of yesterday's judges have become household names. Lord Denning, Lord Devlin, Lord Scarman and Lord Hailsham, to name some of the most prominent, are known to the general public. But that public has little idea of how they or their successors work. The media do not always enlighten us. The headlines ('Judges Slash Fares', 'Gillick's Bitter Pill,' 'You Fools!') are good entertainment but a poor substitute for understanding. This book therefore seeks to open up the people and the processes of the upper echelons of the judiciary by analysing how judges do, and how they should, make law.

Does it matter anyway? Dworkin's flights of rhetoric answer emphatically in the affirmative – courts are 'the capitals of law's empire, and judges are its princes' and law in turn 'makes us what we are'. I do not share that perspective. I would not claim that law is the centre of the universe. Even within law's limited empire, the courts are not the only important institution. Different tribunals, for example, make tens of thousands of decisions on industrial matters, social security claims and immigration appeals. Hundreds of thousands of legal disputes never come to court or tribunal or any other formal decision-maker. Even when cases do reach the courts, most judges spend most of their time refereeing disputes over facts. These are not simple or unimportant matters. Many books could be written about the manifold functions of the law or of the judges without focusing on the concern of this book. Nevertheless, I have chosen the questions of how judges do and should decide hard cases because the judiciary's law-making role also deserves serious attention within our democracy.

So the remit of this book is limited. It examines what does, and what should, happen when the judges are required to decide a disputed point of law. We are concerned, therefore, with the one hundred or so judges in the High Court, Court of Appeal and House of Lords; more particularly with the Court of Appeal and House of Lords, thirty or so top judges; and most especially with the ten Law Lords, headed by the Lord Chancellor and occasionally supplemented by other peers who have held high judicial office.

It is necessary to emphasize that I do not believe that judges are the be-all and end-all of legal study and endeavour because otherwise we might fall prey to another crippling disease, appellate-courtitis. It is necessary to repeat that the vast majority of judges do not spend the vast majority of their time in making law because the reality is that judges spend more time in applying settled law to disputed facts, so that their skill, like the skill of most lawyers, lies in sifting through a mass of conflicting factual material.

Moreover, we must not exaggerate the law-making role of judges in comparison to that of Parliament. Even with this narrow range of senior judges who *do* have the opportunity to make law, their opportunities to develop the law are far more restricted than are the opportunities for those who can push legislation through Parliament. So this book should not mislead readers into placing undue emphasis on the judges' role.

Nevertheless, in some areas, the top judges do resolve social, moral and political dilemmas. Although Parliament could, and sometimes does, reverse their conclusions, it often finds it embarrassing to controvert the judiciary. Increasingly, Parliament seems pleased to pass the buck to the judges in such areas as sexual morality, where elected politicians fear that any decision on their part will lose rather than gain votes. And in other countries, most notably the USA, the Constitution operates so as to give judges more power to decide the fundamental questions of law. Since there is increasing pressure for the United Kingdom to emulate the USA by adopting a Bill of Rights, the question of judicial law-making deserves analysis now more than ever.

At the same time as some people want to extend, through a Bill of Rights, the influence of British judges in shaping the law, others are increasingly concerned about the kind of judges currently appointed. Shouldn't they reflect a cross-section of the community? Shouldn't there be more women judges (instead of none in the top ten, one in the top thirty and only three out of the top one hundred)? Shouldn't the House of Commons be more involved in their appointment? It is therefore opportune to consider who the judges are, how they work, and how they could be helped to make better law.

In searching for that truth, we must distinguish two lines of inquiry. One question is how *do* judges make law. The other is how *should* they make law. The first is a descriptive question. The second is a prescriptive or normative one. Dworkin claims that his thesis is *both* an accurate description and the ideal prescription. This seems to add to the implausibility of his argument. One might perhaps believe that judges do decide in a certain way, or that they ought to decide that way but, unless one is dreaming, it seems unlikely that they are such paragons of virtue that they are doing exactly what they should be doing. Griffith, on the other hand, does not really have a prescriptive theory at all. He thinks it is futile to say what judges ought to do because they will always decide in the same conservative way. Thus his thesis is only descriptive. His refusal to engage in the prescriptive exercise seems unduly pessimistic. Moreover, all his criticisms suggest that his implicit normative thesis is that judges should decide as he would decide if he had a free hand. That is not much of a prescription, in my opinion, but perhaps it is as near as Griffith comes to a criterion by which to judge judges.

For it is only if we look at both angles that we can establish some standards of what judges ought to do, in order to criticize them for what they are doing. Perhaps it is inevitable in this regard that I will fall into the Dworkin trap of saying that what the judges ought to do is what they are groping towards doing at the moment but which they have so far failed to articulate.

Indeed, my contention is that judges are influenced by three factors but that they rarely address two of them consciously or at least openly. It seems to me that they ought to make explicit what is only implicit at present. To that extent my description and prescription are also similar, but I hope to plead not guilty to confusing what is and what ought to be by showing how we would get better law-making if the issues were faced squarely.

In constructing my account, I hope to offer a framework which is comprehensible and comprehensive. I have chosen to approach my task in two ways: first, by explaining some of the major controversial cases of the last decade; second, and more briefly, by assessing a few of the most well-known judges of the last decade or so. There is a danger in following only famous cases and judges. Such a selection can itself lead us away from reality. Indeed, as I correct the proofs of this book while listening to the argument before the Law Lords in *Spycatcher III* (to which we will return anon), I have just heard Anthony Lester QC (to whom we will also return anon) open his case with precisely this point. He began by quoting an irrelevant case (itself a barristerial tendency to seek support from the past in all things) in which the great American judge and jurist, Oliver Wendell Holmes, warned that great cases, like hard cases, can make bad law. The Holmes/Lester point, like so many Holmes and Lester points, is right. The cases and judges discussed in this book are unusual. Otherwise you would not be interested in them and the media would have ignored them. My sample inevitably involves more scope for creative law-making than arises with a typical case or judge. But these are the most important cases in two respects. First, in that the judges can develop the law. Second, in that our perceptions of judges often rest upon the media coverage of these *causes célèbres*.

Reactions to judgments are predictable. Those who read about a controversial case in their papers will have their assumptions about the judges reinforced partly because some people choose a paper to reinforce their views anyway. But occasionally academics can write something against the run of the paper's editorial policy or, at least, provide some reasons for more sober reflection on judgments. Let me illustrate with a couple of personal examples. In the sterilization case, Professor Ian Kennedy and I wrote an article in *The Times* which was much discussed by counsel and the Law Lords in the following day's argument. Although they did not adopt our preferred analysis, at least judges were prepared to read in court, and in the course of argument, what was being written in the press. In the *Spycatcher* case, there was much media hostility to the Law Lords' judgments, before and after they were published. *The Times*, for example, criticized the majority in its leading article but at least it also printed the full text of all the judgments and published opposite their leader an article by me which tried to explain the reasoning of the majority Law Lords.

These are but small examples of a general trend, namely a breaking down of the barriers between 'academic' and 'journalistic' writing. More important examples would include the doyen of British jurisprudence this century, Professor H. L. A. Hart, who was not above writing for a wide audience in, say, the *Listener*. Professor Dworkin himself published much of his work originally in the *New York Review of Books*. Professor Griffith has contributed many enlightening articles to many left-of-centre magazines. But books are a necessary adjunct to instant commentary. If only to increase the understanding of the press readership faced with an endless stream of cases, it seems necessary to stand back, pull together some themes from a series of spectacular cases and then proceed from a more informed basis. Hence this book aims to provide that perspective. That objective has in turn dictated my choice of familiar cases and judges, building on the intuitive assessment readers will already have made as to the merits of a particular decision or decision-maker.

The task of judicial biography, or prosopography as Professor Heuston has described it, is one which British judges have generally escaped but one which I think should be adopted. I do not have the time or resources to undertake a thorough analysis of all our senior judges at present although I am in the early stages of researching a biography of one of them. But the United Kingdom needs an effective Centre for Judicial Studies and a multi-disciplinary army of researchers to track the attitudes of judges and proto-judges. A few short sketches in this book can do no more than point the way.

That raises the final question for this introductory chapter: which way will this book point?

My descriptive conclusion will be that there are three factors which *do* influence judges but only two of them are regularly acknowledged and argued about by judges and counsel. My prescription is that judges *ought* to focus on all three influences. The first factor is past law, the second is present and future consequences, the third is judicial role perception. These can be subdivided infinitely but perhaps the next useful level of generality is to break the three broad headings into the following six questions:

I Past statutes, precedents and principles
1 What do any relevant statutes say?

2 What do any relevant precedents say?
3 What do any principles which might be said to underlie those rules, or to underlie analogous areas of the law, say?

II Present and future consequences
4 What consequences will flow from the alternative decisions?
5 Which consequences are the most desirable for the law to promote?

III Judicial role
6 Is it appropriate for the judge to allow II to outweigh I or vice versa, given this area of the law, this judge, and the alternatives for law-making by other institutions?

It may be that the theories of Dworkin and Griffith can be accommodated within this framework, and there are millions of permutations within the structure. It is far from being the last word on how to judge judges but I hope it will provide a clear basis on which others will build more complex designs. Nor is it the first word, in that other writers have foreshadowed parts of the framework. John Austin, for example, the nineteenth-century legal philosopher and a disciple of Jeremy Bentham, observed in his lectures on Jurisprudence that a judge's 'decision is commonly determined by a consideration of the effect which the grounds of his decision may produce as a general law or rule'.

My earlier work, *Law and Morals*, overlaps with this aspect of judicial decision-making, the second category identified here. Disputes over the merits of legal alternatives, particularly where there is great interest in the underlying moral controversy (although I claim that there is always such an underlying moral conflict), can be understood as centring on two kinds of disagreements. First, we might dispute the consequences of a legal decision (question 4 above). Second, we might dispute the values by which we judge the consequences (question 5 above). Hence, in the Gillick case, some people had a factual disagreement as to whether the Law Lords' ruling would increase or decrease the chances of teenage pregnancies. Others argued about the relative values to be given to teenage autonomy and parental influence. Some, of course, disagreed over both issues. Some of the judgments in the case itself, however, argued as if this was not the primary concern. They focused on the first factor of what clues and commands could be discovered amongst the previous legal material. Other judgments did take on the consequentialist arguments. Some also passed comment on the role of the judges. Overall, however, no clear pattern emerges from that set of five judgments or from other cases. The three factors are sometimes all set out, sometimes one or two of them are ostensibly ignored.

It is my contention that the second and third factors inevitably intrude into the decision-making process but that the conventions which dictate concentration on only the first aspect lead to law-making by default. We usually get a discussion of the past law but the other influences are often concealed in the judgment. This leads in turn to them being concealed in counsel's argument and so we enter a downward spiral. The thesis of this book is that judges are not only concerned with what has gone on in the legal past, they have to think also about what is going to happen in the future and about their proper role in developing the law so as to resolve any tension between the past and the future. Amazing as it may seem, there is considerable resistance to this simple truth. We must therefore begin by a trip into dreamworld.

Fairy Tales

———

Why do people still believe in judicial fairy tales, noble dreams and nightmares? I do not underestimate the power or the significance of these beliefs. Escapism and fantasy have a place in our lives, so long as they are not confused with reality. But in the sphere of judicial law-making, the tenacity with which people cling to their beliefs is astonishing. One might have thought, for example, that the Nightmare could be dispelled by exposing the fallacy in the argument. Thus Griffith's book, *The Politics of the Judiciary*, was immediately subjected to this criticism by another LSE professor, Kenneth Minogue, who wrote in the *Times Literary Supplement*:

> The logic of Professor Griffith's argument is perfectly clear. It runs: if the courts were politically conservative, they would come down against trade unions; they do come down against trade unions; therefore they are politically conservative. In logic, this is called the fallacy of affirming the consequent, and it is a fallacy because there are usually many different and possibly conflicting propositions from which the consequent might follow.

> In moments of realism, it seems obvious that there are explanations for trade unions losing cases in the courts, such as the fact that statutes might have been passed by a parliament elected on a platform of curbing trade union power, or the fact that trade unions *do* sometimes try to act above and beyond the law. It is also obvious that the courts do *not* always come down against the unions. But Griffith's fallacy of affirming the consequent nevertheless captures the imagination of some students and would survive any number of courses in logic from Professor

Minogue. Some people *want* to believe that this is the key to judicial law-making.

But there is a further curiosity. Even if the students were expecting to be examined by Professor Griffith, they would not revise for their examinations by learning where the judges went to school. If Griffith set an examination problem, in advance of the *Spycatcher* litigation but based on its facts, and asked his students to advise the newspapers on their chances of success, the students would not respond by saying:

> Lord Bridge went to a leading public school, Marlborough, and will therefore decide in favour of the establishment. Lord Templeman is the only Law Lord to have been educated at state schools and will therefore decide against the ruling class.

If they did respond in that way, Griffith would not give them a First. Apart from the fact that their prediction would have been hopelessly wrong since Lord Bridge decided for the press and Lord Templeman for the Government, Griffith would expect reasons based at least in part on the legal merits of the case. Griffith dedicated his book to an Oxford university student, his own son, Ben, but I cannot believe that he would expect such students to regurgitate the thesis of his book without any reference to statutes and precedents.

Even those examined by Professor Griffith would be be more likely to regress from the Nightmare (which, as it happens, I believe has an element of reality lurking within it) in the examination hall and to start repeating fairy tales (which also have an element of truth in them but which otherwise, like the Nightmare, distort reality). Again, some people *want* to believe in the fairy tales. They are comforting, as fairy tales should be, since the goodies win and everyone lives happily ever after. Above all, the message of the fairy tales is clear. That appeals to some who would otherwise find it difficult to come to terms with the reality of our complex legal system.

The basic idea of the fairy tale is, as we have seen, that the judge conjures up the answer to any legal problem through some magic formula. The words used are not 'Open Sesame' but 'the rules of statutory interpretation' and 'the rules of precedent'. The leading authority on the so-called rules of statutory interpretation, the late Professor Sir Rupert Cross, has described these fairy tales in recounting his experience as a tutor:

> Each and every pupil told me that there were three rules – the literal rule, the golden rule and the mischief rule, and that the Courts invoke whichever of them is believed to do justice in the particular case. I had, and still have, my doubts, but what was most disconcerting was the fact that whatever question I put to pupils or examinees elicited the same reply. Even if the question was What is meant by 'the intention of Parliament'? or What are the principal extrinsic aids to interpretation? back came the answers as of yore: 'There are three rules of interpretation – the literal rule, the golden rule and the mischief rule.' I was as much in the dark as I had been in my student days about the way in which the English rules should be formulated.

The fairy tale of statutory interpretation therefore begins with the 'literal' rule according to which judges interpret a statute by giving the words their plain meaning. This is useless advice in controversial cases because there may be no single plain meaning. The next 'rule' is the 'golden rule' according to which judges should apply the plain meaning unless that produces an absurdity. But what is an absurdity? On to the mischief rule which states that judges should look to the purpose behind the Act. Yet again, there is plenty of room for doubt as to what the mischief was.

Moreover, which rule should one prefer in the event of conflict? Suppose the plain meaning conflicts with the purpose behind the Act, should judges defer to Parliament's wording or Parliament's intention? Or should the judges just choose what *they* think makes most sense?

Sometimes, Parliament has not spoken at all on a legal area. The 'common law' of judicial decisions therefore is all the judge has in the way of pre-existing legal text to guide the current decision. The judge might feel freer to depart from the thrust of that past law, as contrasted with cases of statutory interpretation. Since the common law will be contained in perhaps more than one judgment, or in more than one form within the same judgment, and since the earlier case might be different from the present one, the judge will feel that he has a more creative role. He is not presented with a single canonical text as in a statute. He has more room for manoeuvre in deciding exactly what the 'precedent' says. And he can perhaps claim that the precedent does not apply. Moreover, the rules of the game allow him sometimes to overrule the precedent whereas the judge is always expected to pay at least lip-service to Acts of Parliament.

The fairy-tale doctrine of precedent, therefore, begins with the notion that the earlier case is divided into two parts, its *ratio decidendi* (the reason for the decision) and the *obiter dicta* (the incidental remarks of the judge which were not necessary for the decision and so are not binding on future judges). In real life, of course, this fairy tale collapses. *Obiter dicta* are often very important indeed. Even if we focus on the ratio of a case, there are great uncertainties in determining what *is* the ratio. Later judges might well interpret the ratio in different ways. If the judges are split in the result and if the majority judges give different explanations of their conclusions, it will be difficult indeed to extract a ratio from the judgments. One should not exaggerate these difficulties – headnote-writers in the press law reports and in the official law reports always manage to summarize the cases succinctly and their accuracy is seldom questioned. But determining the ratio is not the only creative task for a judge who is trying to decide what the pre-existing law suggests as the answer to his present case.

For, even if the ratio is clear, a judge has further tricks of his trade available before he has to apply it. He might 'distinguish' or 'overrule' the precedent. There is some disagreement on what it means to distinguish a case. The standard view seems to be that you distinguish a precedent by identifying some material difference between the facts in the two cases, so that the earlier precedent does not apply to the present case. Others say that is hardly very surprising. If the cases are not alike, then the force of the adage that like cases should be treated alike has no application. The cases are unalike, so obviously the earlier decision is not a relevant precedent. They suggest that distinguishing means something more significant, namely that distinguishing a case involves *changing* the precedent. The judge in the later case is narrowing down the rule in the earlier decision, by restricting its sphere of application, but he must do so in such a way that would still justify the same result in the first case. Of course, the headnote at the top of the report of the old case remains the same and some would say that a later judge cannot change the ratio of the earlier decision. But even they would admit that a later judge can change the importance of the earlier precedent by undermining its logic or narrowing its sphere of application.

Distinguishing in either sense is a power which all courts will possess but its power is limited. It only allows judges to restrict the impact of earlier cases, not to expand them. In contrast, the power of overruling is possessed by fewer judges but to greater effect. The rules as to who should follow whom when they can find no way of distinguishing are as follows. Courts should follow higher courts. The High Court therefore follows the Court of Appeal and the Court of Appeal follows the House of Lords. This makes sense if one believes that the better judges gravitate, or rather levitate, to the top of the judicial hierarchy and if they have more time for reflection on points of law. But does a court have to follow an earlier decision at its own level? The High Court does not have to follow itself. The Court of Appeal is supposed to follow itself except in rare circumstances. The House of Lords used to claim that it was bound by its earlier decisions but has now freed itself through a Practice Statement in 1966 so that it can overrule itself. If there is anything more obvious than the Griffith fallacy, it is the Dworkin fallacy that judges do not make law, given this Practice Statement which clearly envisages the senior judges departing from their earlier decisions. Even if there are no 'gaps' in the law because, as Dworkin believes, there are principles underlying the law, that does not mean that judges never make law. Making law is not just about settling unsettled issues. The Law Lords undoubtedly can make law through the technique of overruling their own previous decisions, in effect by unsettling settled law.

The power of overruling, therefore, is judicial law-making at its most powerful. But in other circumstances, judicial law-making will appear in more subtle forms. Judges can shield behind fairy tales by claiming that they are only interpreting statutes or only following precedent. But the reality is that in hard cases they have considerable scope for creativity. They can use different canons of construction to reach different results as to what a statute means. They decide for themselves what is a precedent and whether they will circumvent it.

This is not to say that judges have as much power as the House of Commons in law-making. First, Parliament can choose its topics whereas the judges have to wait for problems to arise in litigation before them. Second, the judges' developments will be incremental and subject to restriction by later judges and/or by Parliament itself if the judges are too bold, whereas Parliament can change the law dramatically and with sovereign power. On the other hand, the impact which any single back-bench MP can have on the law is not that great as only one individual out of 650 in the Commons. One judge out of a bench of three or five may make more of a mark than a back-bencher, if less than a Cabinet Minister.

I do not propose to dwell any longer on the detail of the fairy tales about precedent and statutory interpretation. The minutiae of the 'rules' can be found elsewhere. They are important for many easy cases. Everyday life in the practice of the law often involves looking at a statutory phrase which has never been tested in court and applying the 'literal' rule, perhaps with a dash of 'mischief' or a 'golden' touch. But in the hard cases which are, by definition, the ones which reach the Court of Appeal and the Law Lords, the answers are not to be found by these rules of statutory interpretation, nor by elaborate tests as to what is the ratio of an earlier decision. Our senior judges are not performing a mechanical task. When they are asked to define words such as 'table', these rules are not decisive. In a 1987 case, the unusual Court of Ecclesiastical Causes Reserved, which comprises bishops and Lords Justices of Appeal, had to decide whether a Henry Moore sculpture could constitute a holy 'table'. The court allowed an appeal from the first instance decision, in which a table was said to require legs, and the result can be seen in the church of St Stephen Walbrook in London. One of the judges said the task reminded him of Plato's *Republic*, while one of the bishops confessed to experiencing some difficulty in following 'the philosophical argument put forward by counsel for the archdeacon concerning the concept of tableness'.

So the judicial resolution of hard cases involves a creative process of interpretation. I shall several times refer to Lord McCluskey's metaphor as providing the most evocative analogy:

> The law does not have the quality of a railway timetable with predetermined answers to all the questions that human life, man's wickedness and the intricacies of commerce can throw up . . . The law, as laid down in a code, or in a statute or in a thousand eloquently reasoned opinions, is no more capable of providing all the answers than a piano is capable of providing music. The piano needs the pianist and any two pianists, even with the same score, may produce very different music.

The truth which this striking passage reveals was vividly demonstrated by the debates over the nomination of Judge Robert Bork as a Supreme Court Justice in 1987. The Senate rejected Judge Bork for a variety of reasons which we shall explore in a later chapter. But one of the most important question marks against Bork's legal techniques was his fondness for the so-called doctrine of historical or original intent. His opponents took great pains to show that this judicial philosophy was no philosophy at all. Bork was accused of believing in the fairy tale that the intention of the framers of the Constitution was a valuable guide for the modern judge. The most dramatic challenge along these lines was laid down by none other than Professor Dworkin. It is undoubtedly easier to cast out the fairy tale of another man's dreams than to acknowledge your own dream-world but it is now time to turn to the Wonderful World of Dworkin.

3

Dworkin's Noble Dream

———

Dworkin has been described by Hart, with due apologies to Shakespeare, as 'the noblest dreamer of them all'. Dworkin's latest book dreams so nobly that it seems to contain more references to British theatre than to British courts. Even the title sounds as if it were destined for the big screen; *Law's Empire* would be a worthy sequel to the Oscar-winning *The Last Emperor*. Indeed, the prestigious *Yale Law Journal* has already reviewed the book as if it were a film in an article entitled 'Indiana Dworkin and *Law's Empire*', a review in which our hero is teased and pastiched. The opening credits are given as 'Written, directed and acted by Ronald Dworkin'. Indiana Dworkin is described as 'a juristic adventurer of international fame and fortune' giving his own version of 'The Greatest Legal Story Ever Told'. *Law's Empire* is depicted as 'Indiana Dworkin's first full-length feature film'. It is 'bound to be a massive box-office success. It is an action-packed, stand-'em-up-knock-'em-down extravaganza.' In more sedate fashion, I have reviewed the book for the *Oxford Journal of Legal Studies*, comparing and contrasting the reaction to the book with the Hans Christian Andersen fairy tale about the Emperor who has no clothes.

In the fairy tale, an Emperor is fooled into believing that he is wearing a cloak spun of the finest thread. The Emperor is also led to believe that the cloak's special property is that it cannot be seen by the foolish. Fearful of the Emperor's scorn, his courtiers are too afraid to speak the truth. If they dare to say that there is no cloak, the Emperor will condemn them as stupid. So they play the game and admire the yarn. It takes an innocent young boy to see the obvious and exclaim that the Emperor is wearing no clothes.

Perhaps we should have second thoughts about the apparent blindness of jurisprudential reviewers who praise Dworkin's cloak of integrity. We should take the place of Andersen's little boy who has the innocence to look at the facts undaunted by the reputation of the Emperor and without fear for his own position. We might then begin to wonder whether Dworkin is streaking through the jurisprudential stratosphere wearing no clothes or, at least, wearing no clothes which were made in Britain.

For, although Professor Dworkin's latest book is called *Law's Empire*, to the extent that Dworkin thinks he is describing Law's *British* Empire, the sun sets on page two. Dworkin makes a frightful mess of discussing English cases in this book, to the extent that it is difficult to believe he has read some of the cases he uses. On page two, for example, his first venture into English legal history is embarrassing. Dworkin takes two examples 'chosen almost at random, from English legal history' to illustrate his belief that his concern with judges has significance beyond his native USA: 'The Supreme Court is the most dramatic witness for judicial power, but the decisions of other courts are often of great general importance as well.' He refers to a nineteenth-century decision which is perhaps studied more in American law schools than in the British law faculties, and then comes up to date with the *Crossman Diaries* case, which he describes thus:

> In 1975 the House of Lords, the highest court in Britain, laid down rules stipulating how long a Cabinet officer must wait after leaving office to publish descriptions of confidential Cabinet meetings. That decision fixed the official records that are available to journalists and contemporary historians criticizing a government, and so it affected how government behaves.

The footnote reveals that Dworkin thinks he is describing *Attorney-General v. Jonathan Cape Ltd. [1975]*, commonly referred to as the *Crossman Diaries* case. Where has Dworkin gone wrong? Well, the case never reached the House of Lords, the highest court in Britain. Oh well, what difference does a court make between friends? Was it the next court down the legal hierarchy, the Court of Appeal? No, the case was in fact decided at first instance in the Queen's Bench Division by Lord Chief Justice Widgery. Ah, perhaps that is the problem for Dworkin,

'Lord' suggesting to the uninitiated that the judge was in the House of Lords. Anyway, so what if Dworkin gets the court wrong in making his choice from the treasures of English legal history, is his point not still valid?

No, Dworkin has not only misread or failed to read or failed to remember which court was deciding, he has also misread or failed to read or failed to remember the content of the judgment. For someone who stresses the distinction beween rules and principles in the rest of his work, it is extraordinary for Dworkin to claim that the court 'laid down rules'. The court was, on the contrary, concerned only to apply principles to the particular case: 'It is evident that there cannot be a single rule governing the publication of such a wide variety of matters.' Even if the judge had laid down rules stipulating how long a Cabinet officer must wait after leaving office to publish descriptions of confidential Cabinet meetings, that would not have 'fixed the official records that are available'. Perhaps there Dworkin is thinking of the thirty-year rule about official Cabinet papers or perhaps he thinks that Crossman's personal, unofficial diaries were official records. Whatever he thinks, he seems to be comprehensively wrong in his account of the *Crossman Diaries* case.

Dworkin has other minor problems with the detail of legal life on this side of the Atlantic. For example, he makes much of his special word-processor package in the preface to *Law's Empire*. but it suffers from a spurious 's'. Thus, in *A Matter of Principle*, he persists in calling John Griffith 'John Griffiths' and in *Law's Empire* he starts calling the Court of Appeal 'the Court of Appeals'. This is like calling Dworkin 'Dworkins' and his favoured court 'the Supremes'.

But, to be fair to the professor, we should look at a case to which he pays considerable attention in *Law's Empire*. The book focuses on four cases, three American and one British. The British case is *McLoughlin v. O'Brian*, a 1983 decision of the House of Lords to extend tort liability for nervous shock to close relatives of those injured in an accident who saw the victims shortly afterwards. This case marked Lord Scarman's introduction of his own brand of Dworkinian jurisprudence into our law. Not surprisingly, Dworkin therefore finds it to be a convenient example to illustrate his thesis.

But Dworkin discusses a schematized version of *McLoughlin*, at no point referring to the detail of the judgment, or the pre-existing law. Yet before we can accept or reject Dworkin's use of *McLoughlin* to support his thesis, we need to know something about the leading case at that time. The general approach to adopt in negligence cases was *Anns v. Merton*. An understanding of this case would have explained to Dworkin's readers why the judges in *McLoughlin* were talking in terms of principle and policy. In *Anns*, Lord Wilberforce set out to post guidelines for judges in future negligence cases:

> First one has to ask whether, as between the alleged wrong-doer and the person who has suffered damage there is a sufficient relationship of proximity or neighbourhood such that, in the reasonable contemplation of the former, careless-ness on his part may be likely to cause damage to the latter – in which case a prima facie duty of care arises. Secondly, if the first question is answered affirmatively, it is necessary to consider whether there are any considerations which ought to negative, or to reduce or limit the scope of the duty or the class of person to whom it is owed or the damages to which a breach of it may give rise.

This test was widely referred to as combining the neighbour-hood principle with policy factors which might limit its appli-cation. But Dworkin has his own special definitions of principle and policy which are of great importance for his account of judicial law-making. For Dworkin, judges do and should 'rely on arguments of political principle that appeal to the rights of individual citizens . . . [rather than] . . . arguments of political policy that claim that a particular decision will work to promote some conception of the general welfare or public interest'.

We must pause to consider why Dworkin thinks this distinc-tion, based on stipulative definitions, is important. The reason is that it provides a neat functional justification for judicial law-making in a democracy since unelected judges are insulated from majoritarian pressures and better able to protect individual rights where they are under threat from considerations of collective welfare. Or, rather, it would be a neat theory if rights were always able to trump collective welfare considerations. Since Dworkin admits that sometimes the public interest can outweigh such rights, presumably judges still do and should consider how significant the policy factors are, and so the simple distinction and the exclusion of policy begins to crumble. But to the extent that the theory remains intact it suits Dworkin's aim of justifying the activism of the Supreme Court in the US Constitution. Democracy rests on a tension between respecting the wishes of the majority (for which we have elected politicians determining policy) and protecting the rights of the minorities (for which we have judges relying on principle). Those who criticize the Supreme Court for usurping the role of the elected politicians are therefore misguided, according to Dworkin. Each institution of government has a separate role to play in American democracy. Principle is what judges are good at discovering and what others cannot be expected to follow.

This seems attractive, if tenuous, in the American setting but unintelligible when Dworkin transplants it, as he tries to do, to this side of the Atlantic. For the problem of democratic legitimacy only arises in the USA since the Supreme Court has the last say in interpreting the Constitution (unless two thirds of Congress and three quarters of the state legislatures support a Constitutional Amendment). Since the judges have more power than the elected politicians, their role does need some explaining. But in the UK, Parliament is supposed to be sovereign and the judges are therefore in a different relationship to the politicians. The judges are not trumping the elected representatives of the people. They are stepping into their shoes where Parliament has not provided a definitive answer to a legal problem, and they know that if Parliament does not like their solution, it can find the time to overturn the judges' answer. Hence the British judges are more like deputy legislators whereas the American judges are like super legislators. What is appropriate for one may not be suitable for another. In Dworkin's language, since Parliament will consider policy, why shouldn't the judges anticipate that process and perhaps save legislative time?

Returning to *Anns* and *McLoughlin*, Lord Scarman in the latter case seemed to reject the balancing act required by Lord Wilberforce in the former case. Lord Scarman says that,

Policy considerations will have to be weighed; but the objective of the judges is the formulation of principle. And, if principle inexorably requires a decision which entails a degree of policy risk, the court's function is to adjudicate according to principle leaving policy curtailment to the judgement of Parliament . . . If principle leads to results which are thought to be socially unacceptable, Parliament can legislate to draw a line or map out a new path . . . Why then should not the court draw the line, as the Court of Appeal manfully tried to do in this case? Simply, because the policy issue where to draw the line is not justiciable.

What Dworkin fails to emphasize when praising Lord Scarman is that the other judges were horrified by these sentiments. As Lord Edmund-Davies observed,

In my judgement, the proposition that 'the policy issue . . . is not justiciable' is as novel as it is startling. So novel is it in relation to this appeal that it was never mentioned during the hearing before your Lordships. And it is startling because in my respectful judgement it runs counter to well established and wholly acceptable law.

As it happened, both Lord Scarman and his colleagues reached the same result in the particular case but nobody bar Dworkin would want to claim that this isolated passage from Lord Scarman had by this stage elevated his US doctrine into British judicial practice. Undeterred, however, Lord Scarman returned to the theme in *Sidaway v. Royal Bethlem Hospital Governors*, a 1985 decision on informed consent. Again, all the Law Lords agreed in the result, given the facts of the particular case, but this time there were significant disagreements on the proper rule of law to apply in other cases. Lord Scarman, bloodied but unbowed after *McLoughlin*, asserted that 'in matters of civil wrong or tort courts are concerned with legal principles; if policy problems emerge, they are best left to the legislature: see *McLoughlin v. O'Brian'*. Presumably, he meant see his own speech in *McLoughlin*. I think we must also see the vehement criticism of his approach by other judges such as Lord Edmund-Davies. Even if we content ourselves with Lord Scarman's speech in *Sidaway*, I suspect that he is so confident of the rightness of the principle which he seeks to draw from the law (and which the others dispute) because he has, perhaps subconsciously, weighed up the policy factors and found them unconvincing. My own view, however, is that the proper answer to poor policy arguments is good policy arguments not an abdication from the controversy.

Lord Scarman apart, Dworkin's rights thesis found little support among the British judiciary. As I have suggested, his ignorance of British law may account for the judges' scepticism. But in *Law's Empire*, Dworkin paints a very attractive picture of the judges as chain novelists engaged in a common enterprise of linking the past to the future by fine-tuning the legal system so as to ensure the consistent application of principle. This is such a beguiling picture for judges to believe in that they may gloss over Dworkin's weakness on real law.

Dworkin's failure to address substantive legal disputes in this country is a pity because his analyses of American law have been invariably compelling, informative and influential. His failure to show any knowledge of any British law cannot but detract from what purports, in part, to be a description of that law. Dworkin introduces *McLoughlin*, after all, in a section entitled 'The Real World'. He has various aims in mind but his chief hope is that his account of this case and of three American decisions,

> will provide, in a more general way, some sense of the actual tone and texture of legal argument. This last reason is the most important, for in the end all my arguments are hostage to each reader's sense of what does and can happen in court.

Yet British law students would be very poorly served if they relied on Dworkin's description of *McLoughlin* for their 'sense of the actual tone and texture of legal argument'. Their sense of 'what does and can happen in court' will surely differ from that provided by Dworkin's reporting.

I have considered in some detail the one British case on which Dworkin concentrates. I have done so because it is in the analysis of real cases that we can see the benefits, if any, of theories of adjudication. More importantly, if students see no benefits in the application, they will doubt whether there is any merit even in the pure theory. Thus Dworkin's failure to examine the detail of British law leads many students to assume that his theories are themselves failures. The standard reaction, which I have seen in many an exam script, runs something like this:

> The trouble with Dworkin is that one doubts whether the theories really determine the results. For a start, he gets the British law hopelessly wrong. What's more, his theories are so malleable. He made a great fuss in *Taking Rights Seriously* and *A Matter of Principle* about the distinction between policy and principle. In *Law's Empire* he makes a great fuss about the distinctions between conventionalism, pragmatism and integrity. He would prefer judges to concentrate on principle and integrity. But the truly herculean judge, let us call her Justice Ronalda, could manipulate any of Dworkin's favoured or despised theories of adjudication to achieve any result in any hard case. The judge who takes account of policy could, and did, decide *McLoughlin* in the same way as the judge who purports to rely on principle. The judge who relies on principle alone in *Gay News* could, and did, reach a conclusion which Dworkin would reject. Similarly, if the SuperEmperor in the Sky forced Justice Ronalda to apply conventionalism or pragmatism rather than integrity, we know full well that she would still conjure up the results which match Dworkin's moral or political convictions. So Dworkin's theories are merely window-dressing. They provide little real guidance to real judges in real cases beyond offering an attractive rhetoric of principle or now integrity.

We know roughly how the Emperor would respond to this line of criticism. In *Law's Empire*, Dworkin includes a section entitled 'Some Familiar Objections' which would intimidate many observers into recanting their testimony and accepting what the eye cannot see, namely that there is a cloak of integrity after all. But even if they were brow-beaten into this admission for the purposes of an examination which a Dworkin disciple was marking, for example, students would not really *believe* that Law's Emperor is fully clothed by the mantle of integrity. For by the time they reach the detailed discussions of conventionalism, pragmatism and integrity, their heart is no longer in the book. Their faith has been shaken by what they have seen with their own eyes, namely that Dworkin has no time for even the basics of British law.

Nevertheless, the failure to apply his theory in the British context is not destructive of the force of Dworkin's theory, so we need to turn to his approach to judicial law-making in *Law's Empire*, where there is a more complex picture of judicial law-making than he has hitherto provided. Dworkin puts up and then knocks down two accounts which he dubs conventionalism and pragmatism. He then develops his own theory of law as integrity.

My objection to all this is not quite the same as the students' scepticism. I believe that, as with all good fairy tales, there is a moral truth lurking in Dworkin's *Law's Empire* and perhaps even a legal truth. My concern is that Dworkin's level of explanation of what is going on within our legal system is pitched at too high a level of abstraction to assist the resolution of real cases. The professor of physics might be able to make sense, to his own satisfaction, of the sound waves produced by a pianist, but a professor of music, or a professional musician, would in all probability be more helpful to the pianist.

But every lawyer and proto-lawyer would benefit from a serious struggle with Dworkin's despised theories of conventionalism and pragmatism. Dworkin points out their deficiencies in *Law's Empire*. This is not a difficult task since he has invented these Justice Aunt Sallies. Conventionalism says that judges are bound by the past law until a gap is reached at which point they are completely unconstrained, while pragmatism says that past decisions are always irrelevant, the criterion for judges being to decide always in the best interests of the community. And lawyers will certainly benefit from consideration of Dworkin's preferred theory, that judges should adopt integrity as their lodestar, seeking to justify their decisions by 'trying to find, in some coherent set of principles about people's rights and duties, the best constructive interpretation of the political structure and legal doctrine of their community'.

Conventionalism is the idea that law consists of statutes and precedents which convention dictates should be followed wherever possible. But where there is no easy answer from this pre-existing law, conventionalists believe that there is a gap in the law which judges can fill as they think fit. My difficulty with this is that the two parts of conventionalism do not necessarily fit together. One can believe that law consists of statutes and precedents without thinking that where the law runs out there are no clues at all for the judge on how to proceed. Indeed I am quite prepared to dub statutes and precedents as 'law' and other factors as non-law but still to insist that judges should, on these definitions, take account of some 'non-law', viz. the consequences of their decisions.

Pragmatism is the view that judges can and should decide not on the basis of pre-existing law but solely on the forward-looking consideration of what the judge thinks will be in the best interests of the community. My difficulty with this is that I am not clear why a judge on this side of the Atlantic should reject pragmatism when he is really acting *in loco* Parliament which *would* take account of such policy factors. Indeed, putting these two derided theories together will strike many as an attractive option with the result that where the law is certain, judges should follow the statutes and precedents but where the law is unclear they should follow the pragmatic search for the most beneficial consequences. I find even this too deferential to the past, personally, since I would have thought it obvious that the 1966 Practice Statement, in which the Law Lords freed themselves to overrule past decisions, allows our top judges to trump past principle with a new rule which will lead to better consequences in the future.

Nevertheless, Dworkin attacks his anti-theories of conventionalism and pragmatism with his customary incisiveness. He observes, as against his own account of conventionalism, that judges do not give up on the past law in hard cases. They try to find analogies. As against his own account of pragmatism, he observes that neither do judges ignore the past law altogether and operate solely on the basis of a utilitarian calculus for the future.

These are good points against false targets. At least they are good points if one believes that judges are doing what judges say they are doing. Dworkin rather naively accepts that at face value here although elsewhere he will reinterpret what judges say to accord with what they do or what he thinks they are doing.

Judges instead are supposed to be motivated by Dworkin's concept of law-as-integrity, trying to fit their decisions into a seamless web of principles which justify existing statutes and precedents. Well, I am all for integrity, even when it seems to be a catch-all for more or less everything that is good in judicial thought. I am not clear, however, on the detail of this grand scheme. I am not convinced that there is a set of values which can consistently resolve all the manifold moral and political dilemmas which underlie the law. Still less am I convinced that judges could discover such a treasure-trove even if it existed. The Noble Dream seems to be collapsing into its close companion, the fairy tale.

Still, on the way to an unconvincing conclusion, Dworkin treats us to some clever theorizing and even to some acute analysis of cases (American ones, that is). Dworkin as limousine liberal, or rather as the Concorde conscience, is pre-eminent in exposing the values with which we should assess the law, even when he creates the impression that it would be improper for judges to evaluate the consequences of a decision. Dworkin as culture vulture cannot resist the literary analogy, considering it at length in *A Matter of Principle* and again in *Law's Empire*. The judge, you will recall, is a chain novelist. This strikes me as remarkably unhelpful. Chain novels are not a plausible or common genre. The theatre director is a better analogy and one which Dworkin uses to great effect (at least for the benefit of those readers who are familiar with Jonathan Miller's various interpretations of Shakespeare). Other performing arts provide further points of reference. From the world of music, for example, Dworkin might think of judges as conductors and Lord McCluskey thinks of them as pianists. Those of us who prefer sporting imagery, on the other hand, might regard judges as fulfilling a less exciting role. The eagerness with which leading QCs forgo the stimulus of fighting Bar Wars for the boredom of the Bench is a mystery to those who see it as akin to Ian Botham becoming an umpire.

At that more prosaic level, perhaps the message which Dworkin is trying to convey is best captured by the idea that judges are the scriptwriters in law's soap opera. They have to keep faith with the characters and their history as laid down by the creators of the series and earlier scriptwriters. But they will try to make sense of that past while developing the plot and the people. Sometimes they make a nonsense of what has gone before when they are motivated by extraneous considerations, as when the *Dallas* scriptwriters brought Bobby Ewing back from the dead and dismissed a year's episodes as Pam Ewing's dreams (a mix of ignoble and noble ones). Even if this is the best analogy for Dworkin's purposes, I somehow doubt whether the professor will regale us with stories of *EastEnders*, *Coronation Street* and *Brookside*, as his tastes incline towards Shakespeare and Dickens (although Dickens produced his novels in serialized form).

But, whatever the literary or artistic analogy, a problem with the whole exercise is that there is a vital difference between soap operas and courts. The decisions of judges affect real lives. They must keep faith with justice, not necessarily with a long-since-deceased scriptwriter's sense of continuity.

Nevertheless, there is an attraction in playing Dworkin's games which it would be churlish to deny. Dworkin talks of judges as Hercules, as chain novelists, as artistic directors, others talk of them as pianists, perhaps we could think of them as the high priests of the law (indeed, that is how they started in ancient Rome). If any of these theologians are genuine fundamentalists, believing in the literal decisiveness of an authoritative text, they are fooling themselves just as much as those who believe in the judicial fairy tale.

Dworkin has indeed set us off in a potentially exciting, if perhaps diverting, pastime. We can build upon and improve on his analogies and question whether they are appropriate analogies. But at some point we have to ask: so what? And what is sad is that Dworkin has never joined in applying the various analogies to help resolve real problems within the British legal system. Admittedly, we lack a journal like the *New York Reveiw of Books* in which much of Dworkin's best work was originally published as he analysed the American cases and issues of the day. But if Dworkin could command here the acreage he receives in that organ, then we could have a constructive, persuasive, deep analysis of cases as they unfold in this country. That is what we need for the judging of judges. We need a dialogue between the judges and the judged. Before that can happen, however, we have to move on from fairy tales and Noble Dreams to more realistic theories. Of course, we might return later if we agree with

Dworkin 'that every decision in a hard case is a vote for one of law's dreams'. But first, we will have to dispose of another surreal account of judicial law-making. We must proceed from the Noble Dream to the Nightmare.

4

That Man Griffith and his Nightmare

———

The most radical dent to the judges' image came with the publication of John Griffith's book, *The Politics of the Judiciary*. Griffith is delighted to be able to quote the response of an aggrieved Lord Denning: 'The youngsters believe that we come from a narrow background – it's all nonsense – they get it from that man Griffith.'

And indeed his book has been influential. It deserves, as Griffith ruefully reflects in the Preface to his third edition, more serious treatment than it has hitherto received from those who doubt its conclusions. There is, of course, nothing new in Griffith's idea that the judges never apply settled law, that they can always make it up as they go along. The American Legal Realists seemed to believe this in the 1920s and 1930s. Griffith's nightmare has been imagined before. But it is interesting that the Left in British politics has given the myth a nasty twist. The judges are not only able to make up the answer, on this interpretation, but they do so in accordance with their class interests. I have dubbed this the Tory Benn thesis: because judges are old, white, rich, upper-middle-class, educated at public school and Oxbridge, just like Tony Benn, they therefore all think in the same, Conservative and conservative way, just unlike Tony Benn. Surely this is too simplistic a view of judicial psychology? Anyway, let Professor Griffith speak for himself. He claims that the senior judges 'have by their education and training and the pursuit of their profession as barristers, acquired a strikingly homogeneous collection of attitudes, beliefs and principles, which to them represent the public interest'.

This judicial conception of the public interest has three aspects, according to Griffith: 'It concerns first, the interest of the State (including its moral welfare) and the preservation of law and order, broadly interpreted; secondly, the protection of property rights; and thirdly the promotion of certain political views normally associated with the Conservative party.'

Griffith concludes that

> Judges are the product of a class and have the characteristics of that class. Typically coming from middle-class professional families, independent schools, Oxford or Cambridge, they spend twenty to twenty-five years in successful practice at the bar, mostly in London, earning very considerable incomes by the time they reach their forties. This is not the stuff of which reformers are made, still less radicals.

The only concession to the judges is that this thesis does *not* impute malicious motives to them: '. . . I mean to absolve them of a conscious and deliberate intention to pursue their own interests or the interests of their class.' But the thesis does seem to fall foul of the logical fallacy of affirming the consequent which we have already encountered. It does seem to assume, mistakenly, that judges have homogeneous views. It does seem to assume, mistakenly, that judges always agree with one another. It does seem to assume, mistakenly, that they always decide for the Conservative government. It does seem to assume, mistakenly, that the interests of the State, its moral welfare, the preservation of law and order and the protection of property rights are all dangerous values to be associated solely with the Conservatives. It does seem to assume, mistakenly, that cases involve one class against another. In short, Professor Griffith's nightmare thesis can be countered with a simple response:

> The political Left have a regrettable tendency to jump up and down with a Thurber-like frenzy, all the more unconvincing for being transparently synthetic, when the establishment behaves as the establishment always behaves. Highpitched complaints that the Law Lords had delivered 'political' judgments show a simple misunderstanding of the role of the judiciary in this country . . . The judiciary are not a collection of muddle-headed old buffers out of touch with the real world.

Who said that? None other than John Griffith himself, writing in *Marxism Today* (February 1982, p.30) about the final decision in the Fares Fair case. Griffith had, incidentally, predicted that the Law Lords would overturn the Court of Appeal, when writing in *New Society*. He had detected a trend of restraint in such cases as *Duport Steels v. Sirs*, where the Law Lords had rebuked the Court of Appeal for a decision in the steel strike. Griffith felt that the Law Lords would similarly draw back from the Court of Appeal stance in the GLC case. He was wrong. Indeed, it is difficult to be one hundred per cent accurate in predicting the outcome of litigation since judges do *not* conform to any simplistic thesis. They do not always follow their class interests.

In this case, surprisingly, Griffith went wrong in reneging on his general approach. But what is Griffith trying to do in his normal role as scourge of the judges, criticizing their decisions? Is he intending to change the world? He certainly does not have any suggestions for improvement. He is pessimistic, feeling that the conservatism he detects is endemic to the judicial role. But he is alerting us to what he sees as a problem, even if it is insoluble.

Yet Griffith is merely saying that he disagrees with the decisions. One gets the impression that he would almost always decide the opposite way, against property, stability, the Conservative party, etc. But would this be preferable? Would it be more democratic? Even if we accept Griffith's argument about the interests which the judges reflect, given that the Conservatives had won elections and therefore were the elected government, what is so wrong with judges deferring to that viewpoint? More strongly, do we have to accept that premise? Does the evidence really show that judges act in this way? Is law really explicable in terms of class interests?

Let's consider a day in the life of the law. On 17 October 1985 Derek Hatton, the deputy leader but primary spokesman of Liverpool City Council, accused the courts of class bias. The High Court ruled that Liverpool council's 90-day notices of redundancy to 5,000 teachers were illegal. The class bias gibe is part of a Pavlovian reaction on such occasions. Mr Hatton went on to allege that, 'Clearly the Tory Government is behind the scenes using the law courts to usurp the powers of democratically elected councillors.'

But where is the class bias in a court protecting jobs at the request of trade unions in the face of a council which has set an illegal rate? Was the democratically elected Tory Government really behind the scenes? What a coup that would have been for a government which at the time had long been at loggerheads with the union which brought the action, the National Union of Teachers. The NUT were not, in any event, seeking to usurp the councillors' powers but were rather seeking to keep the councillors within their legal powers.

Mr Hatton is not the only loser to attribute class bias to the judges. But the allegation is simplistic, naive and misguided. Nor, incidentally, did it stop Mr Hatton subsequently using the courts to compel the Labour party to follow a fair procedure in its examination of his involvement with Militant Tendency. His victory in the courts is a good example of the fact that litigation is often conducted between members of the same class. Militant Tendency takes the Labour party to court, unions take Labour councils to court, working miners take striking miners to court and companies take other companies to court.

Even when there is a legal battle between different classes or between the Right and the Left, it is by no means true to say that the Hatton cynicism is always justified. The present Tory Government, for example, has suffered many defeats in the courts over social security, rate-capping and transport, some even at the hands of the GLC which the Government was in the process of abolishing.

Judges do not all think alike. Nor can all judicial issues be reduced to class-based or Right/Left terminology. On the same day that Derek Hatton lost in the High Court, Victoria Gillick lost her campaign against teenage contraception in the House of Lords. The judges in her case clearly did not think alike. The first-instance judge's decision was overturned by a unanimous Court of Appeal and then an appeal against their decision was successful by a 3-2 majority in the House of Lords. There was so much disagreement that 5 of the 9 judges who heard the case actually supported Mrs Gillick but she lost because she failed to muster a majority at the last crucial stage.

Nor is it obvious whether the ultimate decision was conservative or liberal. Were the majority Law Lords being conservative in deciding for the establishment, the DHSS and the medical profession? Or were they being liberal in acknowledging children's rights to contraception? At least some cases are too complex and unrelated to class for any judge who wanted to be class-biased to be confident which side his class supports.

This critique of the Griffith thesis applies even more strongly to the facile approach of many others who criticize the judges for their background. A 1987 *Labour Research* document, for example, purports to put the 'judges on trial'. It has 'examined' the background of 465 judges, although I suspect this means that it has skimmed through *Who's Who*. The Report comes to six stunning conclusions, to which I add my own observations in parentheses:

1 'The overwhelming majority of the judges come from a highly privileged section of society' (a background they share with the overwhelming majority of Labour Cabinet Ministers, senior civil servants, professors, etc.).

2 'They are not young – more than one in three (166 of the 465) are at least 65 years of age' (wow, let us know when man bites dog or when teenagers become judges, again age is a factor they share with at least some leading Labour politicians and trade unionists).

3 'They are overwhelmingly male – only 17 of the 465 are women' (admittedly scandalous but not out of line with the percentage of women in the House of Commons).

4 'They are overwhelmingly white – indeed there is only one of the 465 judges who is black' (overwhelmingly strikes me as an understatement; again this is a genuine scandal but again, at the time this was published, January 1987, this was a better record than the House of Commons, 0 out of 650).

5 'A sizeable minority have been actively involved in politics' (well, none of the Law Lords had been an MP or candidate, none of the Court of Appeal had been an MP and only one, now retired, had been a candidate – albeit a Fascist candidate in the 1930s – and of the High Court judges, 1 had been a Conservative candidate, 1 a Liberal candidate and 2 Labour candidates – does this prove that those top judges who have strong political views are twice as likely to be radical left-wingers as Conservatives, or does it simply prove nothing?).

6 'There are four judges of white South African origin' (but some

of my best friends are white South Africans of impeccable liberal, radical, socialist and non-racist credentials; they should not be condemned for their origins, nor should these judges).

The Report goes on to allege that 'Nine out of ten judges went to public school and eight went on to attend Oxford or Cambridge.' Lord Mackay went to Edinburgh and they are unsure what happened to Lord Bridge. In fact, he did not go to university. Perhaps because that does not fit the thesis, it is mentioned that he went to Marlborough, which the Report describes as 'a reasonable start in life'. Lord Keith, who they seem to think is of Kinkle rather than Kinkel, is criticized for saying that trade unionists are 'privileged persons', while in the next sentence they have to admit that he was appointed by a Labour Government. The final indictment in the Report is that 'All appointments to the House of Lords (as to the Court of Appeal) are made on the advice of the Prime Minister after consulting with the Lord Chancellor'. This is indeed the theory but in practice it is the Lord Chancellor who decides. So what is *Labour Research*'s grand conclusion?

Overall the *Labour Research* survey reveals that the judges come from a very narrow section of society. Inevitably they reflect the aspirations and values of the rich and powerful whose hobbies, recreations, clubs and educational backgrounds they share.

But does it? And does that show any impact on their professional decision-making? And what should we do about it? It seems that the logical fallacy of affirming the consequent, which we encountered in an earlier chapter, has lost none of its hold over some sections of the Left in British politics.

I do not write this chapter in a spirit of hostility towards the Left. On the contrary, my point is that the legitimate complaints of the Left about occasional judicial decisions will never be taken seriously so long as they are submerged in a welter of rhetoric about the background of the judges. At no point is the connection between background and decisions explained. At no point are alternative explanations canvassed. It is foolhardy to dismiss all judicial decisions because of the judiciary's background.

And the Left is inconsistent. Not only have the Tony Benns of this world shown time and again that one can be extraordinarily privileged and yet socialist but also the principal legal guru of the Left in British politics is a product of the same background. Professor Lord Wedderburn's hand is behind many a Labour Government's legislation on industrial relations and behind many a trade union's legal strategy. His word is accepted as law by his colleague, John Griffith, who does not dismiss Wedderburn's sophisticated analysis because Wedderburn had a privileged background.

Just because Wedderburn went to good schools and to Cambridge, and indeed stayed in that bastion of privilege for a decade as a don before joining the LSE, just because Wedderburn, like Griffith and the judges, is a barrister, just because Wedderburn has accepted a life peerage like the senior judges, just because of all this we should not ignore the cogency of Wedderburn's scholarship.

I would go so far as to say that Wedderburn is the outstanding lawyer in the country, who ought to be appointed as a Law Lord even if he is old, white, male, rich, upper-middle-class, good school and Oxbridge. Nobody rivals his appreciation of past law, the impact on the real world of a legal decision and the problems besetting the judicial role. That is why he should be a senior judge. I see no evidence to suggest that his views are determined by his background. Those of us who have not had the well rounded education of Griffith and Wedderburn, do not perhaps know who Thurber is or was, but with that caveat, perhaps we can all agree that it is time for the Left to stop jumping up and down in a Thurber-like frenzy and to cut out the high-pitched complaints that the judiciary are a collection of muddle-headed old buffers out of touch with the real world. Let's shake off our nightmares, stop day-dreaming and grow out of believing in fairy tales. What is the reality of judicial law-making?

Towards Reality

So what is the best way forward? The obvious way to test these myths is to look at some cases. But this is itself a dangerous exercise. Dworkin, for example, is suspicious of 'empirical' evaluation of competing accounts of judicial decision-making. And one realistic legacy of the original Nightmare-sufferers, the so-called Legal Realists, is the warning that we should not just accept whatever the judges say they are doing as the real explanation of what they are actually doing.

Moreover, any selection of cases is itself pre-judging the issue. How do you know whether or not I have picked a 'fair' sample? In this book, I cannot hope to detail sufficient cases to convince you that both thesis (judges never make law) and antithesis (judges always make law to suit their class) are misguided exaggerations. I am convinced that the truth is in the middle but it will take me a lifetime and several books to persuade you (watch this space).

Let me therefore take a dozen cases which will be familiar to you as a follower of current affairs over the past decade or, if you are a student who was still in primary school when some of these cases were news, cases which you will hear about in the course of your studies. I have included some which could most plausibly be explained on a Griffithesque purely class-based political slant and some which seem to be a Dworkinian quest for principle. I hope the selection gives a fair impression even if it is very small and far from scientific. The cases span the last decade and a range of issues.

I will endeavour to show that a variety of factors influence the judges, that it is unfair to blame them on the class argument, that it is utopian to believe that the judges are merely teasing out principles latent in the law, and that it is the height of naivety to suppose that the judges are value-neutral discoverers of the law.

Judges, or at least the top appellate judges, have a creative role. They are influenced in their exercise of discretion by such factors as statutes, precedents, principles of the common law, their sense of justice, their sense of the community's sense of justice, the desire to settle the instant dispute, a wish to explain their decision consistently with the expectations of the legal profession so that it can be used as a precedent, the esteem of their peers, and so on.

I have already suggested, at the end of the first chapter, that these can most usefully be reduced to three factors:

1 past law, precedents and statutes;
2 present and future consequences;
3 judicial perception of their own role.

The first factor is the most likely to be explicitly addressed in a judgment. The second factor is approached more coyly. Counsel tend to look for a precedent with the 'right' policy factors in it, thus sneaking consideration of the future into the balance by ostensibly referring to the past. I should stress at this point that how counsel argue a case is obviously of the greatest importance to how the judges decide it. Alan Paterson's study of the Law Lords has demonstrated this. But this truism is often forgotten by commentators who rush in to criticize the judges when it is in many ways the barristers who have determined the nature of the legal argument. If we are to have more candid judgments, we need more candid arguments by counsel. As for the third factor, it seems to me that the legitimacy and degree of creativity in the judicial function must depend on what other institutions of the state are doing. When Parliament was unrepresentative of the people in the eighteenth and nineteenth centuries, the judges did not need to feel hesitant about stepping into the law-making role. In the twentieth century, however, our notions of democracy in the UK suggest that the courts should defer to Parliament. In the twenty-first century, or perhaps even now, the fact that Parliament is overburdened may mean that the pendulum should swing back towards judges filling the vacuum.

The first factor most obviously involves skills which are traditionally taught in the law schools. The second involves issues of economics and philosophy. The third is a question of political and constitutional theory. Most judgments do not do justice, if you will pardon the expression, to this wide spectrum of concerns. But it is to judgments which we must now turn.

Indeed, since we will be examining judgments throughout the next part of this book, we must reflect on the actual and the ideal purpose of judgments. Fundamental questions, therefore, are why, when and how judges write their opinions.

There is no set pattern to judgments but they usually follow something like this structure: the facts are set out, the legal issue is pinpointed, the previous law is explored, any 'policy' arguments are summarily treated, the law is applied to the facts, the conclusion is reached and an order is made. But is this really how the judge's thought processes work? That would seem unlikely. Judges might well reach a conclusion intuitively and then work backwards to provide a justification. Occasionally, in so doing they might change their minds. They will also sometimes respond to drafts of their colleagues' judgments. In the appellate courts, the judges will often reserve their judgments for at least a little while in which to reflect on how to explain their conclusion. But time does not always permit this and those occasions perhaps provide clues as to how judges make up their minds.

It is at least clear that judges sometimes feel the need to give their conclusion without simultaneously providing the reasons. In the summer of 1976, for instance, the Labour Secretary of State for Education asked the courts to enforce his directions to the new Conservative Council in Tameside. The council was trying to retain some of the area's grammar schools, rather than carrying out the scheme of its Labour predecessors who intended to move to a comprehensive system in that September. The Conservatives had won the May local elections on a manifesto which pledged them to resist such a change. The House of Lords decided in favour of the Conservative Council. As pupils had to be selected for September, the judges announced their decision at the beginning of August after a few days' consideration but they left their reasons until the end of October. This might explain an unusual feature of these judgments, namely that they were remarkably thin on case-law and remarkably fulsome in their treatment of the facts. Perhaps when their Lordships came to rationalize their hunches, they found that the previous case-law did not easily support their views.

The practice of deciding first and explaining later caused problems in the summer of 1986 when the Law Lords held back their reasons for their decision on the legality of the Trustee Savings Bank flotation. The Government acted on the result of the case before the detail of the judgment arrived and was widely held to have acted prematurely. The Law Lords initially said that the depositors had lost their case but when their judgments were later announced, they were widely misinterpreted as also involving a semi-defeat for the Government. In the interim, the Government had already proceeded with the flotation.

Most famously, in the summer of 1986, the Law Lords announced their conclusions on the question of granting an interim injunction against Peter Wright's book *Spycatcher* before they could reasonably be expected to have produced reasoned judgments. When the result and then the reasons were given, the majority Law Lords, who decided against the newspapers who wished to publish details of Peter Wright's allegations, were twice criticized.

These three cases confirm the fact that judges will become convinced of the result in a case before they have worked out the detail of their justification. Judgments are a rationalization or explanation of how the judges have decided. They do not mirror the thought process of the judge. There is no reason why they have to be in their present form. My contention is that the judges could formulate their judgments to accord more closely with their reasoning processes if they acknowledged the variety of factors which influence them.

Lord Denning's propensity to write about his own judicial performance has highlighted a few examples in which he admits that his judgments were misguided. Most interestingly, he once admitted that all the reasons for a decision which were based on the past law were spurious but that he would still like the decision to stand, basing it now on the final paragraph of the original judgment which revealed his forward-looking consequentialist or policy arguments. He explains the 'unguarded statements' in *R v. Secretary of State for the Environment, ex p. Ostler* by saying that the judgment was given *ex tempore*. Judgment was not reserved but given straight after the conclusion of argument. Lord Denning was clearly motivated by the policy factors but sought to cloak this with the legitimacy of precedent. Even without that pretence, however, he would stick to his policy grounds.

That case must support my hunch that precedents are not the whole story and that the perceived future consequences of the case, plus Lord Denning's belief that he was free to manoeuvre the law to suit his vision of the future, were central to the decision. The case involved a small businessman, Ostler – who was, as befits a man of that name, a corn-merchant – and his complaint that a secret deal between Department of the Environment officials and another businessman adversely affected his interests. That agreement had secured the other man's acquiescence in the blocking up of access roads at an earlier inquiry on the promise that his worries would be dealt with later. But that solution involved compulsorily purchasing part of Ostler's property. By the time Ostler realized what was happening, it was too late. He discovered the deal eighteen months later but the relevant statute allowed only six weeks in which to complain. Ostler asked the Court of Appeal to get round the time limit clause. The courts had recently found their way round clauses which purported to exclude them completely from reviewing administrative actions. Denning and co. could easily have done the same here but they chose to 'distinguish' the helpful precedent on the basis of the reasons which Denning later recanted. The Ostler case shows that Denning cannot always be type-cast as the champion of the little man against the state.

All these examples suggest that it is possible to intuit a decision without having to work through all the possible justifications in longhand. When the judges do come to provide reasons, they do not have to follow a particular framework. They might simply ignore inconvenient counter-arguments. They might shelter behind one reason without revealing others.

We would be foolish, therefore, to believe that the written verdicts provide the whole story. What is not said is often as important as what is said. And what the judges do is as important as what they say.

It has to be said that judicial speeches are not in any event models in the art of communication. Part of this is attributable to the legal profession's general tendency to use convoluted language in order to maintain a mystique. Part of it is perhaps because the judges are unsure of their audiences – are they addressing the litigants, their lawyers, other lawyers, academics, the media, the public, posterity, or simply one another. The good communicator presumably tailors the message according to the audience. Many diverse audiences make this a difficult but not impossible task. When it really matters, judges can produce judgments which are comprehensible to all. A notable example of this was the US Supreme Court's decision in the historic 1954 *Brown* case that segregated schooling was unconstitutional. The Chief Justice insisted that the judgment should be unanimous, short, pointed, understandable and capable of being carried by all the press in its entirety and of being read and understood by the whole nation. The Court did produce such an opinion. That should be the model for our judges.

In the pages which follow, we shall see that so far the British judges have failed to produce judgments which fit an appropriate, consistent structure. But we should be able to tease out from the clues they provide what has really been influencing the judges in their law-making. We now turn, therefore, to a selection of cases from the past decade, looking at one for more or less every year. We will begin with some brief accounts, often imagining how Dworkin and Griffith might react to the cases. But by the end of Part II we will be more confident, less concerned with Dworkin or Griffith, more interested in a detailed, realistic analysis of the more famous recent cases.

Part II

Cases

———

6

Gay News

———

Our first case was decided in 1979 when the House of Lords heard an appeal from a private prosecution brought by Mary Whitehouse against *Gay News*. The newspaper had published a poem and picture depicting Christ as a homosexual. The editor and the publishers were convicted of blasphemous libel for 'vilifying Christ in His life and in His crucifixion'.

Griffith does not mention the *Gay News* case at all and Dworkin only refers to it in passing (in footnote 15 to p. 234) and in a cavalier fashion. According to Dworkin,

> The disagreement between Lords Diplock and Edmund Davies, on the one hand, and Lord Dilthorne (*sic*) on the other, in the notorious blasphemy case *R v. Lemon* [1979] 1 All ER 898, illustrates the importance of not ignoring this connection between changes in popular morality and the boundaries of local priority. The former insisted that the law of blasphemy be interpreted to reflect development in other parts of criminal law; the latter that blasphemy, for some unexplained reason, be counted an isolated domain of its own.

But much more could and should be said about this case. Dworkin seems to have a view on the merits of the decision but he does not explain why. He does not give the uninitiated reader much of an idea of what the case was about.

The question for the Law Lords was not whether it was right for the crime of blasphemous libel to have itself been resurrected (although that might have been a good question) but whether the crime of blasphemous libel required an intention to produce shock and resentment among Christians or whether the crime could be committed by merely intending to publish a poem which had that effect even if the publisher did not intend so to upset others. If the latter interpretation of the law were chosen, the offence would be one of 'strict liability' and thus one could be guilty of it without meaning to offend just because people had in fact taken offence. But if the former interpretation were chosen, then it might render nugatory the offence since it would be difficult to prove.

The senior Law Lord, Lord Diplock, observed that the offence had seemed obsolete for fifty years until this prosecution had been launched. He then gave an account of the history of the law, mentioned the impact alternative decisions would have on society and on future prosecutions, laid down his own views on his own role and concluded in favour of *Gay News*. His judgment was a *tour de force*, encompassing all the factors which I advocate. 1–0 to *Gay News*.

Viscount Dilhorne ignored any talk of the consequences of his decision, did not consider the role of the judges and took a different view of the old law, coming to what non-lawyers might describe as a conclusion which smacks of everything antiquarian within law's reputation: 'I am unable to reach the conclusion that the ingredients of the offence of publishing a blasphemous libel have changed since 1792. Indeed, it would, I think, be surprising if they had.' Although Harold Wilson once remarked that a week is a long time in politics, it seems that 197 years is not a long time in the law. 1–1.

Lord Edmund-Davies gave a long summary of the early law, showed how the early harshness was ameliorated and then how the law became confused. He considered the practical or policy difficulties, said that he considered that the role of the Law Lords would allow them to change the law to what he thought it already was if his interpretation of the past was disputed, and joined Lord Diplock in deciding for *Gay News*. 2–1.

Lord Russell gave a short speech which said that 'The authorities embrace an abundance of apparently contradictory or ambivalent comments. There is no authority in your Lordships' House on the point. The question is open for decision.' This shows that the analysis of the past law was not decisive. In a sense, of course, that must be true for all decisions by the Law Lords since they have the power since the 1966 Practice Statement to overrule their own previous decisions. In another sense, it is probably true for many appeals to the Lords since the case would not be pursued if the law were obvious. So how does Lord Russell decide? His judgment is cryptic, to say the least, but his argument on the policy behind the offence seems to be that the point of the law prohibiting blasphemous libel is to stop people being offended, so if the offensive material is published that is that. 2–2.

The result therefore hinged on the views of the junior Law Lord, Lord Scarman. As we shall see, Lord Scarman is widely regarded as the most liberal of British judges. He tends to escape criticism from the Left who accuse judges of being conservative. Which way would he decide? For *Gay News*? No, he joined Lords Dilhorne and Russell:

> My Lords, I do not subscribe to the view that the common law offence of blasphemous libel serves no useful purpose in the modern law. On the contrary, I think there is a case for legislation extending it to protect the religious beliefs and feelings of non-Christians. The offence belongs to a group of criminal offences designed to safeguard the internal tranquility of the kingdom. In an increasingly plural society such as that of modern Britain it is necessary not only to respect the differing religious beliefs, feelings and practices of all but also to protect them from scurrility, vilification, ridicule and contempt.

Lord Scarman continues by making it very clear that he has a vision of his proper role as a judge. He realizes that he cannot extend the law in the way which he has recommended since that would be a task for the legislature. But he insists that he has a right, indeed he says a duty, to 'state the law in a form conducive to the social conditions of the late twentieth century rather than to those of the seventeenth, eighteenth or even the nineteenth century'.

He surveys the earlier law to conclude that 'historically the law has required no more than an intention to publish words found by the jury to be blasphemous. Yet I recognize that another view, such as that developed by my noble and learned friend, Lord Edmund-Davies, has great persuasive force. Indeed, it has the formidable support of my noble and learned friend, Lord Dip-lock.'

So, Lord Scarman has one view of the past law but he is not content to rest there, particularly as he realizes that senior and distinguished colleagues disagree on his interpretation. What next?

'The issue is, therefore, one of legal policy in the society of today.' In the rest of his speech, Lord Scarman seems to argue that the protection of the religious feelings of citizens is a necessary way forward for a plural society. Hence game, set and match to Mrs Whitehouse, with *Gay News* losing 3–2.

With the exception of Lord Dilhorne, there is an openness in these judgments which transcends their disagreements. The other four judges acknowledge the power they have to develop the law. They realize that there is no simple matrix which determines whether past cases trump future consequences, nor are there simple answers to the questions of what the past law says, what the future consequences will be or whether those consequences are desirable. They do seem to admit that if they were so moved, they could trump the past by reference to the future. Of course, they disagree on the answers to those questions. But I would contend that their disagreement with Lord Dilhorne is more significant and I have no hesitation in preferring their view. At the prescriptive level, my justification is that this will conduce to better, more informed law-making because all the implicit factors are being made explicit and therefore susceptible to argument. At the descriptive level, how can I be sure that the other four better capture the existing practice? Four to one is not a bad ratio but, more fundamentally, the issue is not what the judges say they are doing but what they are actually doing.

This case is mentioned only in passing by Dworkin, and not at all by Griffith. It is my impression that both would have joined the minority of Lord Diplock and Lord Edmund-Davies but I cannot pinpoint why. It may be that Dworkin would have some sympathy with Lord Scarman's sentiment but I would have thought he would regard Lord Scarman as wandering well away from the principles which underlie the law. Griffith might consider it more 'establishment' to facilitate prosecutions for blasphemous libel and so also join the dissent, although I have never been clear why values such as law and order, the defence of property or, as here, the protection of religious sensibilities, should be regarded as the preserve of one class.

Anyway, my point is that we do not know what the critics have to say because they have not addressed this crucial case and I suspect that they will have some difficulty in reconciling their flawed methodology with their substantive political views. Just like judges, of course, academics are juggling past law and future consequences so as to reach their conclusion on the rights and wrongs of a case. But academics usually allow themselves the luxury of allowing the consequences to trump the past law and the delight of choosing their cases in the first place. They often have underdeveloped senses of the problems of operating within the constraints of fulfilling a role. Like judges, they often dress up conclusions on consequences as resolutions of conflicts within the past law.

On all these counts, the split 3–2 *Gay News* decision is a good touchstone of how the self-appointed judges of judges operate. I do not exclude myself from these strictures against academics. Trying to be as honest as I can, I think I would have sided with Lords Diplock and Edmund-Davies. I admire their openness about the judicial process in this case and, for what it is worth, I share their analyses of the past law and their hunch that the world will not fall apart even if the draconian impact of the offence of blasphemous libel is mitigated by the requirement of proving a specific intent. But then I also admire Lord Scarman's response to all these points. In choosing between them, I would have to admit that the balance is tilted by my hunch that Lord Diplock was the best lawyer on the court and Lord Edmund-Davies was the best, indeed the only, criminal lawyer on the court. Is that a proper consideration?

7

Steel Strike

———

The steel strike of 1980 provides our next example. This case, *Duport Steels v. Sirs*, illustrates dramatically the fact that judges have stark disagreements about their proper role. This was one of those cases which seemed legion in my days as a student, namely those in which Lord Denning in the Court of Appeal got into trouble with the House of Lords.

Bill Sirs led the steelworkers' union, the Iron and Steel Trades Confederation, into a strike against the British Steel Corporation in January 1980. Then the union sought to extend the strike to the private steel sector. Duport Steels Ltd and other private steel companies therefore sought an interim injunction from the High Court to prevent the strike going ahead and interfering with their business. They argued that the union was not in dispute with them but with British Steel.

The first-instance judge, Kenneth Jones J, declined with some reluctance to grant those injunctions because he felt constrained by a decision of the House of Lords which interpreted section 17 of the Trade Union and Labour Relations Act (1974) as amended. The Law Lords had already interpreted that section as meaning that if trade unionists honestly believe they are acting in further-ance of a trade dispute by extending the strike, then they cannot be prevented from doing so.

The Court of Appeal sat extraordinarily on the Saturday morning, the next day, and overturned the judge's refusal to grant an injunction. The Court of Appeal, led by Lord Denning, considered that the steelworkers were not really in a trade dispute with their employers, British Steel, but with the Government. The Court of Appeal tried to get round the previous decision of the Lords and the statute. They also pointed to the policy considerations. As the Master of the Rolls Lord Denning observed,

> To call out these private steelworkers, who have no dispute at all with their employers, would have such a disastrous effect on the economy and well-being of the country that it seems to me only right that the court should grant an injunction to stop these people being called out tomorrow morning, to stop all this picketing and to stop all these people who are preventing the movement of steel up and down the country.

The next week saw the Law Lords convening at short notice to hear an appeal, which they readily allowed. A month later they gave their detailed explanations which included many a rebuke for Lord Denning and many an observation on the role of judges in a democracy. The first factor, in my terminology, the past law, was clear. Any policy factors did not come into play in these circumstances. The third consideration, the role of the judges, was firmly resolved in favour of allowing the first to trump the second. Lord Diplock, for example, said:

> My Lords, at a time when more and more cases involving the application of legislation which gives effect to policies that are the subject of bitter public and parliamentary controversy, it cannot be too strongly emphasized that the British Constitution, though largely unwritten, is firmly based on the separation of powers: Parliament makes the laws, the judiciary interpret them. When Parliament legislates to remedy what the majority of its members at the time perceive to be a defect or a lacuna in the existing law (whether it be the written law enacted by existing statutes or the unwritten common law as it has been expounded by the judges in decided cases), the role of the judiciary is confined to ascertaining from the words that Parliament has approved as expressing its intention what that intention was, and to giving effect to it. Where the meaning of the statutory words is plain and unambiguous it is not for the judges to invent fancied ambiguities as an excuse for failing to give effect to its plain meaning because they themselves consider that the

consequences of doing so would be inexpedient, or even unjust or immoral. In controversial matters such as are involved in industrial relations there is room for differences of opinion as to what is expedient, what is just and what is morally justifiable. Under our Constitution it is Parliament's opinion on these matters that is paramount . . .

It endangers continued public confidence in the political impartiality of the judiciary, which is essential to the continuance of the rule of law, if judges, under the guise of interpretation, provide their own preferred amendments to statutes which experience of their operation has shown to have had consequences that members of the court before whom the matter comes consider to be injurious to the public interest.

Lord Keith of Kinkel joined in the same spirit:

The one public interest which courts of law are properly entitled to treat as their concern is the standing of and the degree of the respect commanded by the judicial system. Involvement in political controversy, particularly in the legislatively governed field of industrial relations, is calculated to damage that interest. In the interpretation of statutes the courts must faithfully endeavour to give effect to the expressed intention of Parliament as gathered from the language used and the apparent policy of the enactment under consideration.

Lord Scarman's judgment explicitly takes up the challenge of examining the third factor of the role of judges in our democracy:

Below the surface of the legal argument lurk some profound questions as to the proper relationship in our society between the courts, the government and Parliament.

In the field of statute law the judge must be obedient to the will of Parliament as expressed in its enactments. In this field Parliament makes and unmakes the law. The judge's duty is to interpret and to apply the law, not to change it to meet the judge's idea of what justice requires . . . Unpalatable statute law may not be disregarded or rejected, merely because it is unpalatable . . .

Within these limits, which cannot be said in a free society possessing elective legislative institutions to be narrow or constrained, judges, as the remarkable judicial career of Lord Denning MR shows, have a genuine creative role. Great judges are in their different ways judicial activists. But the Constitution's separation of powers, or more accurately functions, must be observed if judicial independence is not to be put at risk. For, if people and Parliament come to think that the judicial power is to be confined by nothing other than the judge's sense of what is right (or, as Seldon put it, by the length of the Chancellor's foot), confidence in the judicial system will be replaced by fear of it becoming uncertain and arbitrary in its application. Society will then be ready for Parliament to cut the power of the judges. Their power to do justice will become more restricted by law than it need be, or is today.

Now, the vehemence of the Law Lords' criticism of the Court of Appeal suggests that there is more to this case than meets the eye. At first blush, the Left would have some difficulty in explaining this case. It does not seem to fit the Nightmare, first because the judges disagree, second, because the ultimate result was a resounding victory for the trade unionists. Perhaps this is why the case seemed to put Griffith off his stride. Before we accept the Law Lords' analysis at face value, however, let me suggest a more cynical interpretation.

First, bear in mind that the Law Lords must have known that the new Conservative Government, led by Mrs Thatcher, was about to introduce a bill into Parliament to rectify the situation which so annoyed the Court of Appeal. The Law Lords made clear their dismay at the state of the law but insisted that their duty was to follow it not to misinterpret a statute. Yet they knew that within months the statute would be rewritten by Parliament in the way which the Court of Appeal had advocated. So the long-term consequences were not as they might appear from the judgments. The decision would only affect this dispute and if this dispute caused chaos, so much the better in the terms of the public appreciating the need to rewrite the law. The long-term consequences for industrial relations would be minimal. Hence the preoccupation with the long-term consequences for the judges themselves. By conceding here, the judges would have a powerful case to hold against Griffith and co., without losing much of substance in the battle against union privilege. Indeed, Lord Scarman's judgment seems to be over-concerned with judicial image and explicitly accepts the need to retrench here in order to fight better battles in the future.

Of course, once we adopt this gloss on Griffith, imagining a worse nightmare than even he suffers from, then the Left's position is as impregnable to argument as is Dworkin's. Internally self-consistent, albeit externally unconvincing, any case could be held to be in the interests of the ruling class because any case will either benefit the ruling class directly or, on this thesis, indirectly by boosting the image of the judges as neutral arbiters in cases where they can afford to 'lose' the immediate issue. I do not myself believe even the soft nightmare, let alone the hard version, but I think that some cynicism is useful in assessing *Duport Steels v. Sirs*. Although the judgments in the Lords ignore consequentialism and maintain that that is beyond their role, my own hunch is that the judges were well aware of the consequences and thus focused on only two out of my three factors in order to gain some general credibility for the judiciary in a hostile climate which thrived on the kind of overt judicial law-making which the Court of Appeal had undertaken.

8

GLC

———

Some of the comments from the Court of Appeal in *Bromley v. GLC*, the 1981 Fares Fair case, lend support to the thesis that judges are affected by their political views. Lord Justice Tasker Watkins, for example, launched an extraordinary attack on Ken Livingstone, the Labour leader of the GLC, echoing Gladstone's words about the true test of a man being power and saying that Livingstone had failed that test.

Moreover, on the surface at least, there seemed to be a marked contrast between the way in which the Labour GLC and earlier Conservative local councils were treated. Whereas Lord Salmon, in the Tameside case to which we have referred, had emphasized the significance of electoral success – 'The Conservative party having won the election in Tameside on 6 May, the authority rightly considered that they had a mandate from the electors to preserve the Tameside grammar schools' – this time the Labour party's mandate to cut fares was given short shrift by Lord Justice Oliver, who said that '[Counsel for the GLC] accepts that whatever other considerations may be taken into account by a statutory body such as the Council in exercising its powers, an advance commitment to, or so-called mandate from some section of the electors who may be supposed to have considered the matter is not one of them.'

The GLC case gives some support to Griffith's thesis, at least at first sight. It is certainly the case to which he devotes the most attention. As I have already indicated, he predicted the wrong result while the case was happening and initially he was restrained in his response. But by the third edition of his book, he was warming to the idea that the GLC litigation proved his point.

I think it certainly proves one of my points that we need our judges to be more explicit about their concerns and to change court procedure so as to facilitate the task of interpreting what politicians meant in enacting statutes. Griffith quotes another academic who has performed a great service in tracing the legislative history of the relevant statute. The fact that this is done after the event shows that it could be done before the judges make their decision in order to inform that decision. Indeed, I suspect that lawyers *do* scour *Hansard* to discover what Parliament really intended in the hope that if it is favourable, they can slip it into the case through some subterfuge.

The issues in the GLC case were twofold: first, what did the statute mean and, second, what were the common-law principles of judicial review?

In interpreting the statute, again the judges should have thought about the practical consequences of their views. Did they fulfil or frustrate the intentions of Parliament? The courts' treatment of the relevant statute left a lot to be desired, the key word being 'economic'. Both the system and the Law Lords were at fault when it came to interpreting the Transport (London) Act (1969). This imposed a duty on the GLC to run an 'integrated, efficient and economic transport' system for London. The Law Lords, with the exception of Lord Diplock, interpreted the key word 'economic' as requiring the GLC to run the transport system, so far as possible, on a break-even basis so that it balanced expenditure with self-generated income. 'Economic' apparently meant 'businesslike'. Yet it has been conclusively demonstrated that the whole thrust of transport policy in 1969 when the Act was passed was to focus on the social cost and benefits of providing public transport, rather than on maximizing profits or minimizing losses. If the courts had looked at the legislative history, they would have discovered that for themselves.

As for the relevance of the mandate under the common-law principles of what administrators should do, it is useful to compare *GLC* with *Tameside*. In *Tameside*, the May 1976 local elections led to a change in educational policy. The newly elected Conservative council reversed the previous Labour council's plan to introduce comprehensive schools. The Labour Government's Secretary of State for Education sought to protect the original scheme by issuing directions under the 1944 Education Act. Section 68 empowered him to do so if he was 'satisfied . . . that any local authority have acted or are proposing to act unreasonably'. The council refused to comply with the directions and the Secretary of State was unsuccessful in an application for *mandamus*.

Five years later, the GLC elections led to a change of transport policy. This time Labour won control from the Conservatives. The new GLC levied a supplementary rate to finance a 25 per cent cut in London bus and underground fares. The Conservative council of the London Borough of Bromley challenged this successfully and the levy was accordingly quashed.

In each case a unanimous Court of Appeal, presided over by Lord Denning MR, was upheld by a unanimous House of Lords, presided over by Lord Wilberforce. Both the Tameside local authority and the GLC referred to their manifestos as they sought to justify their actions before the courts. Broadly speaking, this argument was favourably received in *Tameside* but not in *GLC*. The obvious conclusion, adopted by Griffith, for example, is that the political complexion of the councils influenced the judges. If we look carefully enough, however, at the pre-existing law and the facts of the case, perhaps there are significant differences which could justify the different approaches of the judges in the two cases.

Lord Brandon, for example, summarizes the law in a way which can help us to reconcile the two cases when he says:

> It is, of course, entirely appropriate for a council, the majority of whose members have been elected after setting out a particular policy in their election manifesto, to take into account, and give considerable weight to, that circumstance when exercising their discretion in relation to that policy after they have been elected and come to power. It would be entirely wrong for such a majority to regard themselves as bound to exercise their discretion in relation to that policy in accordance with their election promises, whatever the cost and other countervailing considerations may turn out to be.

Again, the Left has rushed in to criticize without pausing to examine the detail, drawing simplistic, misleading analogies between cases. The GLC was not being criticized because the councillors considered their manifesto. That was desirable. What was wrong, said the Law Lords, was that they considered nothing but the manifesto. Yet circumstances had changed in between the promise and its attempted fulfilment.

Nevertheless, while the manifesto part of the judgment is not so prejudiced as it has been painted, other aspects of the case are unsatisfactory. Lord Scarman, in resurrecting the fiduciary duty to the ratepayers – a concept which has proved powerful in the subsequent six years but which had previously only appeared once in 1925 and once in 1954 in two cases widely regarded as disgraceful – said, 'so far as I am aware, the principle of a fiduciary duty owed to the ratepayers has never been doubted. Certainly, I do not doubt it.' Yet in the case which gave birth to the idea, the Poplar Borough case, the distinguished Lord Justice Atkin (generally thought to be the outstanding judge of the century) had said in the Court of Appeal, 'My Lords, I venture to doubt the proposition of the court below that there is a fiduciary duty to the ratepayers.' Admittedly, he was reversed in the House of Lords but the dubious origins of this duty should have been re-examined. This is not to criticize Lord Scarman. He had to rely on the arguments presented to him by counsel. Nor are counsel to blame since their aim is to win and they might well have thought that there was no point in pushing various controversial points. What is at fault is a system which does not provide for *amicus* briefs or researchers for the judges (clerks, as the American judges call their research assistants, or *referendaires*, as help European judges).

9

Discrimination

The most basic issue in interpreting the Race Relations Act (1976) is the meaning of the word 'race'. This very question arose in *Mandla v. Lee* in 1983. A Sikh boy applied to a private school which would have accepted him but only on condition that he conformed to the school rules by cutting his hair and not wearing a turban. As an orthodox Sikh, he felt that his conscience would not allow him to do so. His father alleged discrimination. The headmaster argued the case for himself (demonstrating, as did Arthur Scargill in arguing a case for the NUM in which he was complimented by the judge on his presentation, that non-lawyers can grapple with the law) that Sikhs were not a race, so that the Act did not apply. Religious discrimination is not prohibited by British statutes. Would the courts decide that the Sikhs did constitute a race for the purposes of the Race Relations Act?

The county court judge dismissed Mandla's claim and the Court of Appeal dismissed Mandla's appeal against that decision. But the House of Lords upheld a further appeal, so that the final decision was in favour of the Sikh boy: Sikhs were a race for the purposes of the legislation (perhaps this shows that it is not, after all, that easy to win a case as a non-lawyer – Scargill also lost).

I was interested to see how Professor Griffith would cope with this case in his most recent edition. When a unanimous Court of Appeal decides one way and a unanimous House of Lords contradicts them, how can one say that judges are shaped by a common class interest? When a Sikh boy wins a liberal interpretation from the final court of the land, how can the judges be accused of always supporting the ruling classes?

Griffith ducks this issue, condemning the Court of Appeal's condemnation of the Commission for Racial Equality and noting without comment that the House of Lords shared Griffith's strictures. Good for the House of Lords, one might think, even if bad for Griffith's thesis. As an earlier chapter makes clear, of course, a more thorough-going sceptic could say that the Law Lords were letting the Sikh boy win so as to bolster their image of fairness between the majority and minorities in a case which did not matter greatly since the boy was already going to another school and since Parliament would probably have intervened to amend the law if they had decided to put Sikhs outside the protection of anti-discrimination legislation. The case had attracted considerable publicity, apart from its intrinsic interest, because it was one of Lord Denning's last cases before he retired, a retirement precipitated (if that is the right word for someone who was in his eighties) by a controversy on race relations.

The Court of Appeal's approach makes particularly fascinating reading. Their Lordships' approaches to statutory construction are revealing. All the tricks of the trade are used, dictionaries, speculations as to 'the' intention of Parliament and so on. Lord Denning quoted the 1934 *Concise Oxford Dictionary*, which in itself raises the question which dictionary of which vintage should be used to help interpret a statutory word? Lord Denning relied on this dictionary for his understanding of the key word 'ethnic', claiming, 'That is the meaning which I, acquiring my vocabulary in 1934, have always myself attached to the word "ethnic". It is, to my mind the correct meaning. It means "pertaining to race".' I do not believe Lord Denning. In 1934, he was a qualified barrister in his late twenties and had already acquired his vocabulary. But Lord Denning did not rest his case solely on the dictionary. He had a clear idea of the purpose behind the legislation against race discrimination and the inclusion of the word ethnic in the statutory definition of race. Parliament, according to Lord Denning, was ensuring that Jews were protected: 'I have no doubt that, in using the words "ethnic origins", Parliament had in mind primarily the Jews. There must be no discrimination against the Jews in England. Anti-Semitism must not be allowed. It has produced great evils elsewhere. It must not be allowed here.' Then the case hinged, for Lord Denning, on whether Sikhs were an analogous group to Jews. He concluded that they were not. The judgment as a whole suggests that Lord Denning had no sympathy with the complaint on its merits and every sympathy with the headmaster.

Lord Justice Oliver fastened on the element of choice, or rather the lack thereof, in defining an ethnic group, 'I do not believe that the man in the street would apply the word "ethnic" to a characteristic which the *propositus* could accept or reject as a matter of choice.' Sikhs are, like Muslims or Hindus, 'in my judgment groups defined by reference to their religious and philosophical tenets to which anyone may belong but which are primarily composed of persons of Indian birth or descent'.

Lord Justice Kerr agreed that Sikhism is a religion and not a race. Like several other judges, he has a particular liking for the 1972 *Supplement to the Oxford English Dictionary*. He said that this dictionary, in defining ethnic:

> adds that, colloquially in the United States, 'ethnic' can mean 'foreign or exotic; un-American or plain quaint'. So Parliament has used this word in a statute to be interpreted by our courts when across the Atlantic, and perhaps even here, people may already be using it in the sense of saying of someone that, 'He seems a pretty ethnic sort of a guy!'

His Lordship is perhaps not a pretty ethnic sort of a guy, since he declined to give ethnic anything approaching an exotic definition.

The Law Lords, however, took a different line. The Law Lords made little attempt to justify their decision. Lord Templeman also revealed little understanding of the legislation when he began:

> My Lords, the Race Relations Act 1976 outlaws discrimination in specified fields of activities against defined racial groups. The fields of activity in which discrimination is made a criminal offence are employment, education and the provision of goods, facilities, services and premises.

This is utter nonsense, since the Act only has one criminal offence, incitement to racial hatred.

But the main judgment by Lord Fraser is of more interest. He quotes the wise words of Lord Simon in an earlier case:

> Moreover 'racial' is not a term of art, either legal or, I surmise, scientific. I apprehend that anthropologists would

dispute how far the word 'race' is biologically at all relevant to the species amusingly called *Homo sapiens* . . .

This is rubbery and elusive language – understandably when the draftsman is dealing with so unprecise a concept as 'race' in its popular sense and endeavouring to leave no loophole for evasion.

Lord Fraser conjured up seven factors from his imagination (fairy tales, nightmares or noble dreams, depending on your point of view) to determine whether or not Sikhs were a racial or ethnic group but they were clearly chosen to achieve the result he wished: long shared history; common cultural tradition of its own; common geographical origin; common language; common literature; common religion; being a minority or being an oppressed or a dominant group within a larger community (this last factor seems to encompass every group!). For some unarticulated reason, Lord Fraser wanted to protect Sikhs. This seems the noble course but it was not dictated by the pre-existing law. Lord Fraser had more than one eye on the consequences of deciding whether or not Sikhs came within the ambit of the Act.

So Griffith might find it difficult to explain two features of this case. First, the judges at the different levels disagreed, despite coming from the same class and sharing the same perception of the public interest. Second, the final outcome was a decision to extend the law's protection to cover a group who clearly were not members of the ruling elite.

Dworkin might be on firmer ground in explaining Lord Fraser's judgment as an attempt to elucidate the principles underlying the law. But, as the Court of Appeal demonstrated, one could equally come up with principles which lead to the opposite conclusion.

These questions of judicial technique re-surfaced a couple of years later in another case concerning racial discrimination which we will therefore consider ahead of its chronological order.

In *Wheeler v. Leicester* in 1985 the House of Lords again overturned a Court of Appeal decision to do with race. This time, the Court of Appeal majority had supported the Labour council's punishment of the local rugby club in support of the council's anti-apartheid policies. The club's 'crime' was that three of its members had gone to South Africa on an England rugby tour. Although the club sympathized with the council's views, it could not stop the members from going. The House of Lords thought that the council was being over-zealous.

There are one or two passages of particular interest for those who believe that personal prejudices influence the judges. Lord Justice Browne-Wilkinson, dissenting in the Court of Appeal, and Lord Templeman, in the House of Lords, both went out of their way to express their support for the council's anti-apartheid policy. They were at pains to show that their conclusions against the council were in the face of their personal opinions. The council was taking unacceptable means towards an end which these judges considered desirable. Where does that leave Griffith?

Browne-Wilkinson's dissent was Dworkinian, emphasizing the judge's belief in principles such as freedom of expression which he claimed to underlie the legal system. But this approach was disavowed by the House of Lords who agreed with his conclusion but took more conventional routes to it. Where does that leave Dworkin?

I would suggest that the area of race discrimination shows that judges will disagree, in all good faith, on how to interpret pre-existing statutes and precedents, on how to assess the consequences of their decisions, and on their own freedom to supplement the 'intention' of Parliament. The judges are not, contrary to Griffith, strikingly homogeneous in their views. The judges are not, contrary to Dworkin, solely concerned with legal principle. The reality is more complex. Moreover, one reason for that is the deliberate policy of Parliament to leave the judges with difficult questions. The judges do not duck these questions which Parliament ought to have answered. They do not always explain their decisions as fully as I would like. But whatever they are doing, they are not simply perpetuating their class interests or even their personal views. They are, in my opinion, struggling with difficult questions, the answers to which could have been given by Parliament. In the absence of courageous legislators in Parliament, the Law Lords in *Mandla* felt they had to pretend that a religious group, Sikhs, were an ethnic group in order to bring them within the protection of the race relations legislation. If the legislators had been forced to clarify their wishes on the matter, they would surely have reiterated the beliefs of the ministers pushing the legislation through, namely that Sikhs were protected. But this would have created problems with the definition of 'race' which Parliament preferred to ignore.

Critics of the judges often prefer to ignore inconvenient decisions such as the Law Lords' conclusion in *Mandla*. Given that it directly contradicted the Court of Appeal and that the end result was to protect a threatened minority, I would have thought that Griffith, at least, needs to explain this aspect of the case rather than the peripheral criticism of the Commission for Racial Equality which surfaced in the Court of Appeal.

10

GCHQ

The Prime Minister, in her role as Minister for the Civil Service, issued an instruction on 25 January 1984, without consulting staff or unions, forbidding staff at Government Communications Headquarters to be members of trade unions. The Council of Civil Service Unions and some individual employees applied for judicial review and were granted a declaration by Glidewell J that the instruction was invalid and of no effect. The Court of Appeal allowed the Prime Minister's appeal. In dismissing the union's subsequent appeal, the Law Lords held that a prerogative power could be subject to judicial review, that past practice had given rise to a legitimate expectation of consultation, but that this was outweighed by the requirements of national security, the Prime Minister having shown that she had feared consultation would itself have precipitated disruption at GCHQ which was the very worry the Prime Minister was trying to avoid by her instruction.

The Law Lords were undoubtedly bold in developing the law in this case so as to permit themselves to examine the exercise of a power under the 'prerogative'. They were quite adventurous in saying that the past practice of consultation with the unions could generate a commitment to future consultation. But they were timorous in deferring to what amounted to little more than an assertion that national security was at stake.

The position on the first point was well put by Lord Fraser, with whom Lord Brightman agreed. He admitted that 'there is no obvious reason why the mode of exercise of that [prerogative] power should be immune from review by the courts. Nevertheless, to permit such review would run counter to the great weight of authority.' Hence he confined himself to the narrower ground that judicial review was appropriate in the instant case because the prerogative power had been delegated to the Prime Minister under an Order in Council. But the other three Law Lords all thought that the time was ripe to go further. The old law on the prerogative was, according to Lord Scarman, 'overwhelmed by the developing modern law of judicial review'.

This is an example of one legal principle, the law relating to the prerogative, becoming out of line with another principle, that relating to judicial review. The Law Lords saw their role as deciding whether to update the law on the prerogative so as to fit the law on judicial review. Now, the boldness of the decision is perhaps explained by the timorousness of the ultimate conclusion that Mrs Thatcher won because national security was at stake. Once the Law Lords had determined that the Prime Minister was going to win on that point, they had more scope for creativity in the broader question of whether or not to develop the law. Lords Diplock, Roskill and Scarman were, in these circumstances, grateful for the opportunity to correct what they perceived to be an anomaly within the law without having to disappoint a litigant by changing the rules in mid-case in a way which would affect the final result.

Nobody could surely retain their faith in the fairy tale after a case like this in which the Law Lords openly admit their creative role in overriding past law. Dworkin, on the other hand, could find some support for his Noble Dream of law-as-integrity in that the judges looked to develop the law on the prerogative and on natural justice in a way which better achieved consistency with the underlying principles of surrounding areas of law. Griffith might argue that the ultimate victory by the Prime Minister vindicates his thesis that judges are conservative.

But while there are undoubtedly various ways in which the decision could be explained, I would maintain that the judges were juggling my three factors in balancing the past law, an evaluation of the consequences, and a vision of their own constitutional role. The past law on the prerogative was that the courts traditionally did not question the exercise of prerogative discretion by ministers. This had become anachronistic when set against the courts' increasing willingness to review ministerial discretion whose source could be traced back to a statute. The difference in the source between the prerogative and the statute could no longer justify different treatment. But why? The judges must have had some standard by which to judge that the time had come to reformulate the law. They could see that the consequences of leaving the old law intact would be unjust. Ministers could escape review and citizens could suffer unfairness merely because of a technicality.

Yet remember that Lords Fraser and Brightman still had their reservations about the proper role of the judges. Although they acknowledged the force of their colleagues' arguments, they felt that it was not appropriate for judges in this case to stray beyond what they had to decide in order to make a broader point about the prerogative. The other judges, however, had a more expansive vision of their own role in which they were entitled to take the opportunity to overrule past law in order to develop a more coherent future for the control of ministerial discretion.

One might question this perception of the judges' role. After all, the practical effect of the old law was that if Parliament wanted the judges to intervene in a particular area of ministerial decision-making, then it could override the prerogative by passing a statute on the subject and automatically therefore bringing the discretion within the ambit of judicial scrutiny. If Parliament left the prerogative alone, it was at least arguable that Parliament knew that was one way in which to insulate ministers from judicial scrutiny in areas where the judiciary had no expertise or legitimacy. By switching the ground-rules from a source-based test to a test of justiciability, the judges effectively took the power out of the hands of Parliament (which could have changed the source of a minister's power through legislation since Parliament in its sovereignty can always override the prerogative) and gave themselves the responsibility of deciding when to intervene. For it is the judges who determine which powers are 'justiciable'. One can accept that Parliament was not an effective policeman of Mrs Thatcher in the GCHQ dispute without necessarily leaping to the conclusion that judges should adopt that role. It might have been preferable for the judges to have declared that there was nothing that they could do and to have called for Parliament to improve its own procedures.

But the result of the GCHQ case itself was a victory for Mrs Thatcher and again I would have thought that this was best explained as a shrewd appreciation by the judges of the consequences of the contrary conclusion. They did not feel that it was within their role to second-guess the Prime Minister's judgement on matters of national security. That would have embroiled them in an even deeper controversy as to the legitimacy of unelected judges usurping the functions of the elected government. My own view here is that perhaps the judges were *too* restrained on this aspect of the case. After all, they would only have been deciding that the Prime Minister should have consulted the unions, not that she must ultimately allow them to continue in existence.

The *GCHQ* case is another dispute which could be interpreted by any one of a number of theories of adjudication, from the Nightmare to the Noble Dream. Our task, as always, is to decide which theory best captures the determining factors in the judges' decision-making process.

Gillick

———

Victoria Gillick sought a declaration that a Department of Health and Social Security circular was unlawful in that it permitted doctors, in exceptional circumstances, to give contraceptive advice and treatment to under-sixteen-year-olds without parental consent. She lost in the High Court, won a unanimous decision in the Court of Appeal and lost 3-2 in the House of Lords in 1985.

Lord Scarman's judgment celebrates the role of the judge and especially the great judge:

> The House's task, therefore, as the supreme court in a legal system largely based on rules of law evolved over the years by the judicial process, is to search the overfull and cluttered shelves of the law reports for a principle, or set of principles recognized by the judges over the years but stripped of the detail which, however appropriate in their day, would, if applied today, lay the judges open to a justified criticism for failing to keep the law abreast of the society in which they live and work.
>
> It is, of course, a judicial commonplace to proclaim the adaptability and flexibility of the judge-made common law. But this is more frequently proclaimed than acted upon. The mark of the great judge from Coke through Mansfield to our day has been the capacity and the will to search out principle, to discard the detail appropriate (perhaps) to earlier times, and to apply principle in such a way as to satisfy the needs of their own time. If judge-made law is to survive as a living and relevant body of law, we must make the effort, however inadequately, to follow the lead of the great masters of the judicial art.

Lord Scarman's exquisite legal prose would have us believe that the enterprise is the Dworkinian one of searching for a principle underlying earlier cases and then applying it to contemporary reality. But there are many different ways of rendering the principle. Perhaps there is more than one principle available for the great judge to discover. Perhaps the great judge is discovering the principle he wants to discover.

Lord Scarman has made, by my reckoning, six attempts to articulate the principle in different parts of a long judgment. He seems to regard each formulation as representing the same principle:

1 The principle of the law, as I shall endeavour to show, is that parental rights are derived from parental duty and exist only so long as they are needed for the protection of the person and property of the child . . .

2 The principle is that parental right or power of control of the person and property of his child exists primarily to enable the parent to discharge his duty of maintenance, protection, and education until he reaches such an age as to be able to look after himself and to make his own decision . . .

3 The underlying principle of the law was exposed by Blackstone and can be seen to have been acknowledged in the case law. It is that parental right yields to the child's right to make his own decisions when he reaches a sufficient understanding and intelligence to be capable of making up his own mind on the matter requiring decision . . .

4 The principle underlying [the age of discretion cases] was plainly that an order would be refused if the child had sufficient intelligence and understanding to make up his own mind . . .

5 The principle is clear . . . we can agree with Cockburn CJ as to the principle of the law – the attainment by a child of an age of sufficient discretion to enable him or her to exercise a wise choice in his or her own interests . . .

6 I would hold that as a matter of law the parental right to determine whether or not their minor child below the age of sixteen will have medical treatment terminates if and when the child achieves a sufficient intelligence to enable him or her to understand fully what is proposed . . .

Lord Scarman presumably regards these several statements as identical or at least as representing the same principle. But others might think that some of the variations on the common theme are significantly different: (2), (3) and (4) are along the same lines, emphasizing that the child must have sufficient understanding and intelligence to be capable of making up her own mind; but (5) talks of a wise choice and (6) talks of understanding fully what is proposed; (1) seems to be on a different tack altogether, focusing on the need to protect the child.

The various formulations do not necessarily coincide to produce the same result. A girl could be capable of making up her mind (satisfying (2), (3) and (4)) in favour of what others deem an unwise choice (thus not satisfying (5)). There may be a difference between understanding (2, 3, 4) and understanding fully (6). But most seriously there is a potential conflict between (1) and the others. Suppose a girl is capable of making up her own mind but the judges feel that she is making a mistake and that her parents' counter-wishes would actually be in the girl's best interests. A judge could argue under (1) that parental rights are still needed here to protect the child. But under (3), for example, the parental protective role is irrelevant if the child can make up her own mind.

One might distinguish (1) and perhaps (5) as being motivated by paternalism whereas the other statements of principle reflect a confidence in autonomy as the ultimate value which the law should promote.

Even if all of Lord Scarman's variations were identical in their impact, it should at least be clear from all this that the judge can arrive at the same destination by different routes. The concept of consent was not controlling Lord Scarman, propelling him inevitably to a method or result. On the contrary, the judge was controlling the concept of consent, using the idea as a technique to explain, justify and apply his conclusions. Which route and which destination depends not simply on the pre-existing law, our first consideration. They also turn on the weight the judge ascribes to such values as autonomy and his hunches as to the practical consequences of imposing a strict or weak test of capacity.

Even within one of Lord Scarman's formulations there is plenty of room for judicial manoeuvre. We could lay down a strong or a weak test of what is meant by capacity to understand what is involved, pitching the requirement of understanding at different levels. Lord Scarman seemed to place a very high premium on understanding, setting a standard which perhaps very few adults could meet:

> When applying these conclusions to contraceptive advice and treatment it has to be borne in mind that there is much that has to be understood by a girl under the age of sixteen if she is to have the legal capacity to consent to such treatment. It is not enough that she should have understood the nature of the advice which is being given: she must also have a sufficient maturity to understand what is involved. There are moral and family questions, especially her relationship with her parents; long-term problems associated with the emotional impact of pregnancy and its termination; and there are the risks to health of sexual intercourse at her age, risks which contraception may diminish but cannot eliminate. It follows that a doctor will have to satisfy himself that she is able to appraise these factors before he can safely proceed on the basis that she has at law capacity to consent to contraceptive treatment. And it further follows that ordinarily the proper course will be for him, as the guidance lays down, first to seek to persuade the girl to bring her parents into consultation, and, if she refuses, not to prescribe contraceptive treatment unless he is satisfied that her circumstances are such that he ought to proceed without parental knowledge and consent.

Moreover, there is still room for discretion here in the meaning we attach to the verb 'to understand' throughout that passage.

Mrs Gillick could have hailed this emphasis on the difficulty of surmounting the hurdle of consent as a victory for her belief that under-sixteen-year-olds should not be entrusted with this decision. The tenor of the rest of Lord Scarman's judgment, however, suggests that he thought under-sixteens could fulfil his requirements as to understanding and maturity.

One of the dissentient judges, however, interestingly adopts more or less the same test as Lord Scarman's third formulation of common-law principle but with the opposite conclusion as to whether it can be satisfied here. Lord Templeman believes that under-sixteens do not possess such a degree of understanding and maturity. He argued that:

> I accept also that a doctor may lawfully carry out some forms of treatment with the consent of an infant patient and against the opposition of a parent based on religious or any other grounds. The effect of the consent of the infant depends on the nature of the treatment and the age and understanding of the infant. For example, a doctor with the consent of an intelligent boy or girl of fifteen could in my opinion safely remove tonsils or a troublesome appendix. But any decision on the part of a girl to practise sex and contraception requires not only knowledge of the facts of life and of the dangers of pregnancy and disease but also an understanding of the emotional and other consequences to her family, her male partner and to herself. I doubt whether a girl under the age of sixteen is capable of a balanced judgement to embark on frequent, regular or casual sexual intercourse fortified by the illusion that medical science can protect her in mind and body and ignoring the danger of leaping from childhood to adulthood without the difficult formative transitional experiences of adolescence. There are many things which a girl under the age of sixteen needs to practise but sex is not one of them.

But this does not tell the whole story. Lord Templeman has admittedly set a high or unattainable level of understanding. The reason for this seems to be his view that such girls would be best protected, in general, by the absence of contraceptive facilities: 'Some girls would come under pressure if contraceptive facilities were known to be available.' But for his disagreement with the majority on the practical consequences of providing contraception for under-sixteens, therefore, his Lordship might have been prepared to accept a principle of capacity to consent along the lines suggested by Lord Scarman. It is difficult to be more precise on Lord Templeman's view of the common-law principle since his seven-page judgment eschews case-law, only once mentioning a case, *Sidaway*, and then only in passing.

But even Lord Templeman thought there were exceptions to the line he had just taken:

> The position seems to me to be as follows. A doctor is not entitled to decide whether a girl under the age of sixteen shall be provided with contraceptive facilities if a parent who is in charge of the girl is ready and willing to make that decision in exercise of parental rights. The doctor is entitled in exceptional circumstances and emergencies to make provision, normally temporary provision, for contraception but in most cases would be bound to inform the parent of the treatment. The court would not hold the doctor liable for providing contraceptive facilities if the doctor had reasonable grounds for believing that the parent had abandoned or abused parental rights or that there was no parent immediately available for consultation or that there was no parent who was responsible for the girl. But exceptional circumstances and emergencies cannot be expanded into a general discretion for the doctor to provide contraceptive facilities without the knowledge of the parent because of the possibility that a girl to whom contraceptive facilities are not available may irresponsibly court the risk of pregnancy. Such a discretion would enable any girl to obtain contraception on request by threatening to sleep with a man.

In this passage, Lord Templeman seems to come close to Lord Scarman's first formulation. Lord Templeman's priority is the protection of the child and he will focus on parental consent so long as the parents will exercise it in such a way as to protect the child. If parental involvement is impossible or likely to be counter-productive, however, then the protection of the child points towards some other proxy. So Lord Templeman then turns to the doctor.

From the point of view of technique, the second Templeman passage is also interesting for mitigating the effects of requiring a high level of understanding by allowing exceptions. Not only Lord Templeman but also Lord Scarman employed this technique, so even if we adopt a restrictive approach based on Lord Scarman's list of what a girl must understand, we can turn to the passage which immediately precedes that and which invokes exceptional circumstances as a ground for dispensing with the requirement of consent (or, at least, as allowing the doctor to act as proxy in giving consent):

> . . . I would hold that as a matter of law the parental right to determine whether or not their minor child below the age of sixteen will have medical treatment terminates if and when the child achieves a sufficient understanding and intelligence to enable him or her to understand fully what is proposed. It will be a question of fact whether a child seeking advice has sufficient understanding of what is involved to give a consent valid in law. Until the child achieves the capacity to consent, the parental right to make the decision continues save only in exceptional circumstances. Emergency, parental neglect, abandonment of the child or inability to find the parent are examples of exceptional situations justifying the doctor proceeding to treat the child without parental knowledge and consent; but there will arise, no doubt, other exceptional situations in which it will be reasonable for the doctor to proceed without the parent's consent.

Obviously, the width of the exceptions contributes to the overall picture of the significance of consent. A judge can concoct a mixture of tests and exceptions to suit his vision of how the law should be tackling the problem of teenage contraception. What is important for our present concern is that the previous legal material is not the sole determinant of the strength of the mixture which any particular judge adopts. Although Lord Scarman spoke as if he was searching for something which was latent in the case-law, Lord Templeman, as I have already observed, ignored case-law. Their disagreement is at least as much a disagreement as to the future consequences of their decisions as a disagreement on precedent.

This is not to deny that there may have been some general guidelines in the pre-existing common law which pointed the judges in a particular direction. Nor is it to deny that in this case, the majority better captured the spirit of those guidelines as compared to the minority. Indeed it is significant that the minority did not attempt to counter the majority's magisterial surveys of the common law. Lord Templeman, as I have said, gave up any pretence of analysing the case-law. But what of Lord Brandon?

For the other dissenting Law Lord, Lord Brandon, the question whether contraceptive advice or treatment was lawful 'appears to me to be one of public policy, the answer to which is to be gathered from an examination of the statutory provisions which Parliament has enacted from time to time in relation to men having sexual intercourse with girls either under the age of thirteen or between the ages of thirteen and sixteen'.

Lord Brandon does not explain why he ignores the majority's search for legal principle. Nor does he explain why he disagrees with the majority when they rely on Lord Brandon's own landmark decision in *R v. D.* The dissentient is in the curious position of being the principal authority for the majority.

Nor does Lord Brandon explain *why* the question appears to him to be one of public policy. Even if it is such a question, why is the answer to be found in certain 'statutory provisions'? When other judges invoke public policy, they are sometimes referring instead to the policy of *the common law*. And sometimes they are looking, not to anything in the past, whether statute or case-law, but to the *future* consequences of a decision one way or the other.

Indeed, if Lord Brandon's statutory provisions demonstrate anything, it is that the public policy in common-law terms was probably against his Lordship, so that Parliament *had* to intervene with a statute to override common-law public policy. But where there is, as here, no *specific* statutory guidance for the particular issue in question, would that not leave the common-law public policy intact and against Lord Brandon?

In any event, the statutes which Lord Brandon relies on are those which make sexual intercourse with an under-sixteen-year-old a serious criminal offence for the *man*. Now what is the public policy behind this? As Lord Brandon admits, it is 'that the relevant statutory provisions have been enacted by Parliament for the purpose of protecting the girl from herself'.

Fair enough. But *if* the girl would have sexual intercourse with or without contraception (and the evidence from doctors seems to suggest that girls who ask for such treatment are already sexually active), then 'to protect the girl from herself' must mean, in part, to protect her from the risk of pregnancy followed by teenage motherhood or teenage abortion, and so public policy would surely support the majority against Lord Brandon. Yet his Lordship's response is to *deny* protection to any girl who threatens to have sexual intercourse with or without contraception. Her attitude, he says, is 'tantamount to blackmail . . . which no legal system ought to tolerate, the only answer which the law should give to such a threat is "Wait until you are sixteen".'

Now this is interesting because Lord Brandon is *not* divining what is public policy from statutes but is instead declaring what 'ought' not to be tolerated and what the law 'should' do. Public policy has become a way of converting what you hope the law's response *should* be, into what you claim it actually *is*.

Moreover, by this stage of his judgment Lord Brandon has moved into an analysis of sexual psychology which, speaking as a complete amateur myself, seems to me somewhat less than complete. Lord Brandon announces that 'The inhibitions against the having of sexual intercourse between a man and a girl under sixteen are primarily twofold.' I was not aware of any evidence being submitted about the potentially infinite inhibitions, let alone any assessment of which two inhibitions top the list. What are these inhibitions?

'So far as the man is concerned there is the inhibition of the criminal law as contained in sections 5 and 6 of the 1956 Act. So far as both are concerned there is the inhibition arising from the risk of an unwanted pregnancy.' Lord Brandon concludes that giving contraceptive treatment removes largely the second of these inhibitions and is therefore contrary to public policy. But again, the facts are that those who approach doctors for contraceptive advice and treatment have usually already engaged in sexual activity, so that these inhibitions have already failed.

But the most surprising use of public policy comes when Lord Brandon examines the one crucial statutory provision: section 5(1) of the National Health Service Act (1977). This states that,

It is the Secretary of State's duty . . . (b) to arrange, to such extent as he considers necessary to meet all reasonable requirements in England and Wales, for the giving of advice on contraception, the medical examination of persons

seeking advice on contraception, the treatment of such persons
and the supply of contraceptive substances and appliances.

This has no mention of age limits. If we are really interested in
Parliament's public policy, then this is surely game, set and match
to the DHSS. But, no. Lord Brandon says he 'would interpret the
expression "persons" in s5(1)(b) as not including girls under
sixteen'!

Having rewritten the governing statute so as to deem under-
sixteen-year-old girls to be non-persons, Lord Brandon finally
notes public policy in the sense which perhaps more immediately
springs to other minds:

> My Lords, great play was made in the argument before you
> of the disastrous consequences for a girl under sixteen of
> becoming pregnant as a result of her willingly having
> unlawful sexual intercourse with a man. I am fully conscious
> of these considerations, but I do not consider that, if the
> views which I have so far expressed are right in law, those
> considerations can alter the position.

Here then, Lord Brandon acknowledges a consequentialist strain
of thought in public policy, but rejects it because the conclusion
would be incompatible with the public policy he has controversially arrived at through an individual interpretation of some
selected statutes. One might ask why his Lordship did not instead
jettison his interpretation of public policy when it was clearly
inconsistent with the most relevant statute and the consequentialist aspects of public policy?

Lord Brandon's strange use of public policy thus brought him
to a view which was more extreme than Mrs Gillick's. 'This is
because,' as his Lordship explained, 'on the view which I take of
the law, making contraception available to girls under sixteen is
unlawful, whether their parents know of and consent to it or not.'

Two of the majority Law Lords devoted a paragraph each to
rebutting Lord Brandon's arguments. Lord Scarman's magisterial
opinion dismissed arguments based on alleged criminality or
public policy as 'surprising'. In his Lordship's view:

> It cannot be said that there is anything necessarily contrary to
> public policy in medical contraceptive treatment if it be

medically indicated as in the interest of the patient's health; for the provision of such treatment is recognized as legitimate by Parliament: see section 5 of the National Health Service Act 1977.

Of course, it *can* be said as Lord Brandon has shown, but otherwise Lord Scarman has summarized the position succinctly.

Lord Bridge, interestingly, is able to defeat Lord Brandon on a different public policy tack. While Lord Scarman's source of public policy is the National Health Service Act (1977), which I have dubbed the governing statute, Lord Bridge tackles Lord Brandon on the latter's preferred territory of the criminal law statutes while adding a passing reference to the other, consequentialist, source of public policy. Thus Lord Bridge concluded,

> On the issue of public policy, it seems to me that the policy consideration underlying the criminal sanction imposed by statute on men who have intercourse with girls under sixteen is the protection of young girls from the untoward consequences of unprotected intercourse. Foremost among these must surely be the risk of pregnancy leading either to abortion or the birth of a child to an immature and irresponsible mother. In circumstances where it is apparent that the criminal sanction will not, or is unlikely to, afford the necessary protection it cannot, in my opinion, be contrary to public policy to prescribe contraception as the only effective means of avoiding a wholly undesirable pregnancy.

So where does all this take us? If a judge wishes to rely on public policy, it seems that he has three routes which he can travel. One is to deduce public policy from the common law. A second is to deduce public policy from statutes. A third is to deduce it from the consequences which would follow in the outside world from a decision in the instant case. All these routes have their hazards. In particular, as we have seen, the first two paths are selective and interpretative exercises. Which Acts of Parliament, for instance, are to be the raw material and how is the 'policy' to be extracted from them? And the third route often involves, as in *Gillick*, judges speculating without the benefit of factual evidence or expert witnesses' opinions.

Courts are by no means the best judges of public policy in this third, consequentialist, sense. The English court procedure does not facilitate, at present, inquiries into the impact of a decision. Moreover, if we really wanted *public* policy under this head, then one might further argue that judges are not the best determinants of the public's wishes. To the extent that we are genuinely concerned with the public's assessment of the consequences of a decision – the question whether the community as a whole, or on balance, would be better off – then surely elected and removable politicians are better placed to reflect majority wishes.

Rash assumptions under this consequentialist head of public policy have the further disadvantage, given judicial reluctance to distinguish and identify the different sources of public policy, of bringing into disrepute also those issues of public policy which judges ought to be adept in solving, namely the first two paths of discerning the spirit behind common law or statute.

Perhaps all this explains and justifies Lord Bridge's observation that the court should avoid 'expressing *ex cathedra* opinions in areas of social and ethical controversy in which it has no claim to speak with authority'. The judicial disagreements in *Gillick* certainly highlight the dangers of cryptic reference to, and reliance on, public policy. The phrase 'public policy' is a beguiling one. But we must always wonder what is meant by 'public'. Does the concept mean the policy of *the* public, or a policy of some of the public, or a policy to do with the public, or a policy announced in public, or just a policy? Similarly, the word policy is susceptible to a variety of interpretations. Putting these two words together spells danger.

Nevertheless, it is sometimes justifiable to resort to public policy. Not, with respect to Lord Brandon, as one's first line of attack, and certainly not as a way of ignoring the plain meaning of a statute. But where there are plausible alternative interpretations of the law, public policy can play a useful role. The danger arises if judges allow their normal precision to disappear at the first sight of public policy. We are entitled to have the content, orientation and origin of a judge's public policy spelled out by him in his judgment. In the attempt to enlighten us, of course, the judge might clarify or even change his thoughts on the requirements of public policy.

I have stressed that I do not attribute the exercise of judicial discretion to class bias. So from where do judges derive their conflicting interpretations of public policy? In *Gillick*, as I have said, they did not draw on any evidence, either in the form of facts and statistics or in the form of evidence from medical and ethical experts. The judges are merely offering their own views, the hunches of five wise old men. Any group of five wise old men might have split 3-2, as did the Law Lords, on the public policy to follow in *Gillick*.

There are two reasons for disagreements on such matters of laws and morals. One is starting from different moral premises, intuitions or priorities. The other is concluding with different predictions as to the factual consequences which would follow from a decision. So when the judges rely on public policy in the third, consequentialist sense, their disagreement might be due to a different estimation of the consequences, whether X or Y would actually happen, and/or due to a different moral evaluation of the desirability of those consequences, whether X or Y would be good or bad.

Now, the more we can persuade counsel and judges to articulate these component parts of their public policy views, the more likely it is that we can iron out unnecessary disagreements, woolly premises and mistaken counter-factual assumptions. We should not allow the magic formula 'public policy' to cast a discreet veil over these controversies.

But I am not so naive as to believe that five judges would always agree on public policy, given sufficient information and frankness. That would be to subscribe to the myth that there is such a thing as one public policy on controversial matters. And while I reject Griffith's critique of the politics of the judiciary, I am prepared to adopt his critique of Dworkin's belief in a shared community morality as 'nonsense at the top of a very high ladder'. Nevertheless, I am fully convinced of the need for greater openness about judicial views of public policy.

Greater candour, therefore, is the order of the day. This may in turn benefit the judiciary. Those who criticize the judiciary's politics and stress their unfettered discretion are given aid by judges who rest decisions on the vaguest of public policy grounds. If judges spell out what they mean by public policy, critics might retaliate by saying that judges are quite incompetent to determine what a majority of the public would like the policy to be. But that is not what is meant by public policy in this judicial context. Public policy is either an attempt to extract the spirit behind common law or statute law (for both of which judges have expertise) or an attempt to predict and evaluate the impact of policies in the public domain. Here I doubt the courts' functional competence but realistically the most appropriate decision-making process, Parliamentary decisions based on full research by government and independent inquiries, is often unlikely to happen. Some of these issues are too hot for Parliament to handle, the code-word for this being that there is no available Parliamentary time. So these important decisions of public policy do, in practice, devolve at least temporarily on the judges. And when that happens, I would like judges to accept the burden of deciding public policy in as open and informed a manner as possible.

Lord Bridge tackled the issue head on but for the most part the judges skirted round it in *Gillick*. This, of course, reflects the judges' implicit assumptions about my third factor – their perception of their own role. Lord Brandon adopts the view that the consequences of his decision are not a matter for him to worry about. His perception is that his (bizarre) interpretation of the legal material is the only consideration. Or rather that is what he says. Perhaps we find it hard to believe that he was not influenced in reaching his strained interpretations of statutes by an assumption that the consequences *were* important and dictated his result. Lord Scarman differed in the result but also failed openly to acknowledge the impact of future consequences on his interpretation of past principles. Moreover, the tacit assumptions of what is the proper judicial role are self-perpetuating in that counsel, knowing that Lord Scarman is now (but remember his earlier, policy-based approach in the *Gay News* case) looking for principle and prefers to ignore 'policy' in the manner of Dworkin, will dress up all their best points as principle. Their aim is to win the case, not to insist on intellectual purity and attempt to change a judge's philosophy.

Nobody, to my knowledge, relied on the Nightmare to assert that the judges decided according to their educational or class background (although some did attribute their decision to their gender). Since the judges disagreed among themselves, it would be more than usually incoherent to rely on education, class or sex as an explanation of the result. The fairy tale and the Noble Dream seemed to be given some currency by Lords Brandon and Scarman respectively. But most commentators and most members of the public would instinctively grasp the truth, that the judges' differing hunches as to the desirability of the likely consequences determined the result and indeed the conflict.

If judges themselves acknowledged the influence of consequentialism and of their role models, then counsel could begin to address openly the central issues. I have yet to meet anyone who is particularly interested in what the seventeenth-century cases say about the very recent phenomenon of teenagers being prescribed the contraceptive pill. What worries people is that they disagree vehemently over the best strategy for dealing with early sexual activity. That is how they judged the judges in the Gillick case. That is how the judges probably judged the matter for themselves. Why not admit it?

12

Miners' Strike

A typical scene from the 1984–5 miners' strike was described by Mr Justice Scott in the case of *Thomas v. NUM (South Wales Area)* on 11 February 1985:

> Some 50 to 70 striking miners attend at the colliery gates daily. Six of them are selected to stand close to the gates. The rest are placed back from the road so as to allow the vehicle conveying the working miners to pass. Abuse is hurled at the vehicle and at the men inside. Police are in attendance. This picketing or demonstrating is taking place against a background of high community tension and known anger by the pickets or demonstrators against the working miners. It is taking place not on isolated instances but on a daily regular basis.

Scott J granted an interlocutory injunction to the working miners, the terms of which ordered the NUM area officers to instruct the lodges in question to discontinue organizing intimidatory picketing. Although only an interlocutory injunction, this effectively resolved the case. The strike ended soon afterwards without an appeal or the full trial.

This case seems to provide ample support for *both* the Griffith and Dworkin theses. Griffith would presumably say that Scott J upheld the establishment line, helping strike-breakers and opposing pickets. He was doing the work of the National Coal Board and the Conservative Government, admittedly at the behest of miners. Ah, but isn't that significant? This was an example of intra-class litigation, miner versus miner. The judge would have to decide in favour of one, and why not in favour of those who were trying to get to work without undue harassment?

Well, Griffith's answer might be because the pre-existing law did not justify Scott's conclusion. Nor would Griffith's view of the consequences of Scott's decision justify the judge's approach. And Griffith's view of the role of the judge would not embrace such an innovative judgment in these circumstances.

The first element in our framework, the established precedents in the law of tort, did not help these working miners. A tort involves damaging somebody by breaching a duty imposed by the law. But the learned judge found that the picketing did not quite constitute five torts: it was not assault, obstruction of the highway, unlawful interference with contract, intimidation or 'strict' private nuisance. These nominate torts were, in essence, deemed inapplicable because there was no actual or special damage and/or the wrong person was suing. Some of the torts might well have been actionable at the instance of other plaintiffs, namely the National Coal Board or miners who wanted to work but who were afraid to cross the picket lines. But these working miners were not suffering the kind of physical or financial damage which the law of torts normally protects. They were still going to work.

As the settled law did not help the plaintiffs, Scott J could have said simply 'and so the action fails'. Instead the learned judge took off on a Dworkinian flight to principle:

The working miners are entitled to use the highway for the purpose of entering and leaving their respective places of work. In the exercise of that right they are at present having to suffer the presence and behaviour of the pickets and demonstrators. The law has long recognized that unreasonable interference with the rights of others is actionable in tort. The law of nuisance is a classic example . . .

Nuisance is strictly concerned with, and may be regarded as confined to, activity which unduly interferes with the use or enjoyment of land or of easements. But there is no reason why the law should not protect on a similar basis the enjoyment of other rights. All citizens have the right to use the public highway . . . The tort might be described as a species of private nuisance, namely unreasonable interference with the victim's rights to use the highway. But the label for the tort does not, in my view, matter.

In the present case, the working miners have the right to use the highway for the purpose of going to work. They are, in my judgement, entitled under the general law to exercise that right without unreasonable harassment by others. Unreasonable harassment of them in the exercise of that right would, in my judgement, be tortious.

Scott J discovers in this Noble Dream the principle that the 'law has long recognized that unreasonable interference with the rights of others is actionable in tort'. But while established torts certainly are unreasonable interferences with the rights of others, it does not follow logically that all such interferences are tortious. *Some* unreasonable interference with the rights of others *is* actionable in tort, but some is actionable in contract or equity and property law, while some is not actionable in law at all (so that, to take a different example, the torts of defamation and breach of confidence do not add up to complete protection from unreasonable invasions of privacy by the press).

The important issue is whether or not *Thomas* concerns the type of interests which are, or ought to be, protected by the law of tort. In this context we should note that Scott J conceded, in rejecting the tort of obstructing the highway, that 'the working miners' entry into and egress from the colliery is not being *physically* prevented by the pickets' (emphasis added). So the plaintiffs in *Thomas* were being protected from *mental* stress. Traditionally, the law has been more reluctant to recognize psychological than physical upsets (hence, for instance, the restricted law on slander or nervous shock). Indeed, the law seems generally to encourage a phlegmatic resistance to such pressure.

Even if we were to accept that this type of interest ought to be protected, it would only be in the context of unreasonable interference with the plaintiffs' *rights*, in Scott J's words. On analysis, the right of the plaintiff working miners was not so much a right to work as in fact a right to travel to and from work along a highway. This is merely one aspect of the more general right to use the highway. And this right is not absolute. Indeed, the striking miners were equally trying to use the highway. The right is qualified so as to exclude unreasonable use which obstructs the highway. But what constitutes unreasonable use must turn on what exactly is meant by the right to picket.

All this is another way of saying that there are competing rights to consider. The striking miners' right to picket must be relevant to the decision, either in qualifying the working miners' rights to use the highway or in questioning whether the striking miners have unreasonably interfered with the plaintiffs' rights. Hence the judge accepted that the 'working miners cannot complain of picketing *per se*'. Yet Scott J proceeded to elaborate on the uncontroversial premise that '[t]he legitimate purpose of picketing is peaceful persuasion or the obtaining of information', to reach his conclusion by imagining 'a large number of sullen men lining the entrance to a colliery, offering no violence, saying nothing, but simply standing and glowering . . . [that] would, in my opinion, be highly intimidating'.

Here again we see a judge looking for principle and finding one when he could have found another. Instead of concentrating on the right to work and principles of the law of tort, Scott J could have focused, perhaps equally plausibly, on the right to picket and principles of the law on freedom of expression. This might have led to the diametrically opposite conclusion that striking miners' rights to free speech should not be circumscribed by the sensitivity of working miners who were in any event already prepared to go to work past such pickets.

This opens up the Griffith thesis that perhaps Scott J was subconsciously motivated by his class interest. It is not clear how one could prove or disprove allegations about the subconscious. But even if one accepts the force of Griffith's argument, it is at least arguable that Scott rather than Griffith has best captured the public interest.

It might well be that Scott J has acted in order to preserve values of peaceful resolution of disputes and to prevent violence. One might regard these as laudable, whether or not one agrees with the striking miners. Their means can be questioned even by those who sympathize with their ends. Certainly, the same class was involved. Nevertheless, it would be churlish to deny that Griffith has a point. Moreover, this was not the only case in which the miners lost. But this was a case in which even the judge acknowledged that he was being innovative. In other cases which had a greater influence on the failure of the strike, the judges were often blamed for applying settled principles of law. Parliament was also blamed for Tory anti-union laws although a feature of the failure of the strike was that it was *not* caused by the application of the new laws since the employers declined to implement them. In some cases, then, the judges were deferring to the old law of natural justice and contract when critics wanted them to subvert the pre-existing law to fit the critics' perception of the best consequences. If they had been so bold, of course, they would have been accused of undue activism by others. But in our particular case the judge did seek to develop the law in a bold way and also ran into trouble.

Now why have I been so kind to Dworkin and Griffith as to choose a case which gives each theorist some support? One reason is that *Thomas* shows how judges can use a quasi-Dworkinian approach when they want to be bold *and* how critics can judge judges in a quasi-Griffithesque way when they object to such innovation.

My point is that in all the miners' strike cases, judges would have been fully aware of the strengths and limitations of the past law, the consequences of their decision and the pressure which this was putting on their own role. Although a case like *Thomas* can plausibly be explained by Griffith and by Dworkin, this does not mean that their theories are the best accounts of judical law-making. The very fact that they could each claim some support from *Thomas* itself shows that we are right to regard the law as a cathedral which can be viewed from different perspectves to yield a different picture. If we have to adopt one perspective, I would still contend that my aerial view gives a more complete impression than do the sketches by Dworkin or by Griffith.

13

TSB

We have already mentioned one aspect of the Law Lords' decision in the summer of 1986 on the question who owned the Trustee Savings Bank. It was one of those cases in which the judges announced the result first and gave their reasons later. The result was that TSB depositors lost their claim that they owned the TSB. This was interpreted as a victory for the Government and, in some quarters, as a classic illustration of the Nightmare – the judges, in effect, seemed to be supporting the Government's desire to float TSB shares and removing the last obstacle in the Government's way. The Government did indeed announce that the sale would proceed immediately. But then the full judgments were published and some people began to eat their critical words. Perhaps the judges were not so bad after all. Even though they had decided against the depositors, the judgments were interpreted or misinterpreted as suggesting that the Government's arguments had also failed to persuade the judges. Did anybody own the TSB?

This case is worth considering, therefore, because it concerned a central plank of the Government's programme of wider shareownership and because this politically controversial issue was placed before judges whose conclusions were widely misunderstood. The judges viewed it as a relatively easy case yet their mixture of technical legal argument and casual asides perhaps contributed to the misunderstanding.

The complex legal position was selectively and misleadingly reported, with the result that many people believed the Law Lords said that the state owned the TSB. Even the Government seemed to believe that and sought to explain away the significance of the assertion by distinguishing itself, the Government, from the state. Opposition politicians doubted whether any such distinction existed. There is some irony in all this since the

Government identified the interests of the state and the Government the previous year in the Ponting saga, whereas the Opposition then could see a clear divergence between the two.

But there was no need this time for the Government to invoke such a distinction. The Law Lords did *not* say that the state owned the TSB. What they did say deserves to be read carefully. Whatever the political merits and demerits of the TSB flotation, the Government should not be blamed on the mistaken ground that they were giving away taxpayers' money.

The TSB case arose because depositors were claiming that they owned the TSB. The Law Lords rejected that categorically. Lord Templeman went on to refute the depositors' 'emotive arguments' that if the depositors did not own the TSB, then this implied the TSB assets were in 'limbo'. Not so, argued Lord Templeman. Lawyers would not be surprised at Lord Templeman's reaction. They know full well that our legal system would not tolerate such a 'limbo' in ownership. If all else fails, our law would, as a last resort, place ownership in the hands of the state rather than recognize any such legal limbo. But in the TSB case, we never had to reach the last resort. Parliament had previously directed where the money should go in the event of the closure of a TSB. Those principles could be applied in the admittedly new circumstances of all the TSBs closing, only to reopen under a different structure.

Hence what Lord Templeman actually said was:

> Statutory trustee savings banks and their assets belong to the state subject to the contractual rights of depositors to the return of their deposits and interest *and subject to the powers and duties from time to time conferred and imposed by Parliament on the National Debt Commissioners and the Central Board, both institutions of the state.* [my italics]

Thus the safety-net of state ownership has not been needed when TSBs have been closed. It has always been understood, and it was recently reaffirmed by a Labour statute of 1976 and a Conservative statute of 1981, that the TSB's assets were to be kept within the movement. Both Lord Keith and Lord Templeman, who gave the two judgments in the case, explained this and quoted the relevant statutory provision:

When a trustee savings bank is finally closed, the trustees shall pay over to the Central Board any surplus moneys remaining in the hands of the trustees, after providing for the sums due to the depositors and for any expenses authorized by the bank's rules; and the Central Board may distribute the moneys among such other trustee savings banks as the board think fit.

So any surplus from Lord Templeman's first proviso as to paying back depositors will be subject to his second proviso – it should go to the Central Board for redistribution within the TSB movement.

That, of course, is exactly what happened in the 1985 Act. In order to float the TSB as a public company with shares quoted on the Stock Exchange, the 1985 Act restructured the TSB and there was no place for the Central Board. Parliament was, in Lord Templeman's terms, changing the powers of the Central Board, or rather, ending them. Of course, it could have legislated for the surplus assets to go to the Treasury, just as Parliament could confiscate all the profits of all the clearing banks. Parliament can do anything in legal theory. But in political practice, since the money did not come through taxation it should not be usurped for taxation purposes now. Parliament was surely right to keep within the spirit of previous TSB legislation as to surplus assets, even if it did not keep within that spirit by issuing shares. The clear thrust of previous legislation and the clear understanding of depositors was that any surplus assets should be kept within the TSB movement. The Government can confidently plead not guilty to the charge of giving away state assets in the TSB sale.

Can the judges plead not guilty to the various charges levelled against them? I think that those politicians and commentators who rushed in to criticize the result as a pro-Government decision and who then rushed back to misinterpret the judgments as an anti-Government conclusion certainly ought to plead guilty to manipulating their judging of the judges. The Government was also at fault in not waiting for the reasoned judgments before acting. Furthermore, the Government was inexcusably lax in not understanding the judgments once they were given.

But the judges themselves resolved a classic case of statutory interpretation with a decision which, once understood, is beyond criticism. Where they erred, as so often, was in their presentation. Careless judicial phrases did not cost lives in this example but they did contribute to unfounded criticism of the Government's decision to let the TSB movement keep the proceeds of the flotation. This was a case where there was great political and public interest. The consequences of a decision one way or another would be dramatic in terms of the Government's credibility. The judges should have explained that this was one of those cases where they really did not have to look beyond the clear and often-repeated words of Parliament. They should have explained their conclusions in terms which would have put the matter beyond doubt. Then we could have returned to the argument about the advantages and disadvantages of the share flotation. Its legality should not have become the focus of attention.

This is not an isolated phenomenon. Controversial political matters are increasingly likely to be taken to the courts. A court case attracts publicity. The media can look forward to a result within a relatively short space of time. The judges need to be sensitive to this quest for publicity and the attempt to drag them into politics. Indeed, they are already in politics, although not party politics, if we define politics as the struggle for power. What the judges need to do is to articulate clearly their conclusions, the reasons for their conclusions and the non-reasons which did not influence them. The beguilingly simple question of who owned the TSB raised many questions about the judges' role in our modern world. It is not enough to get the law right. They must get the message right as well. Their repeated failure to do so will be illustrated again when we turn to the *Spycatcher* litigation.

14

Sterilization and Abortion

———

Two cases on issues of great moral concern reached the appellate courts at great speed in 1987. Both cases attracted wide publicity and much criticism for the judges, not all of it well informed or deserved. In the first case, a student sought to stop his former girl-friend from aborting their child. The foetus was of about 20 weeks' gestation. The argument turned on the interpretation of a phrase in a 1929 statute. The father lost. Then the courts were asked to authorize the sterilization of a mentally handicapped teenager. The argument here turned on what was in her 'best interests'. The cases deserve to be considered together because they raise some common concerns, not only about the relation-ship between law and morals, which I have considered elsewhere, but also about the role of the judges, our present concern. Since both cases raced through the courts, we might wonder why we need to have appeals at all if it is not to provide a more considered, less rushed analysis of how the law should be clarified or developed. In particular, is the court process well suited to deciding such difficult matters or should Parliament take up the burden? Since the final judgments in both were somewhat sketchy, again this raises questions about the point of giving reasons. And since the judges seemed to be responsive to media criticism, the further issue is raised – are we beginning to achieve the kind of dialogue between the judges and the judged which I favour?

The judges' analysis of the statutory phrase 'capable of being born alive' in the 1986 Oxford student abortion case, *C v. S*, was dismissed as 'astonishing', 'confused' and a 'mockery' by some pro-life groups. This reaction is code for saying that those pro-lifers would have twisted the law to suit their moral convictions if they had been the judges. But that is one of the reasons why they are not judges. Judges should not subvert the law. We should continue to ask *Parliament* to change the law. We should not bad-mouth the judges when our real quarrel is not even with the statute which they were honestly and plausibly interpreting, but with another statute, the Abortion Act (1967).

Those who accuse the judges of incompetence or malevolence would do better to consider the context of the Infant Life (Preservation) Act (1929). In 1928, Mr Justice Talbot's direction to a Liverpool jury was that, 'It is a felony to procure abortion and it is murder to take the life of a child when it is fully born, but to take the life of a child while it is being born and before it is fully born is no offence whatever.' The following week Lord Darling introduced a Bill to plug this gap between abortion and murder, to protect, in his words, children 'in the course of being born'. Although those words were changed in Select Committee to 'capable of being born alive', Lord Darling emphasized in moving the second reading that, 'It really is a Bill designed to prevent children being destroyed at birth.' The long title of the subsequent Act talks of the 'destruction of children at or before birth' and the offence is termed 'child destruction'.

As this legislative history suggests, it is not surprising that the Abortion Act (1967) section 5(1) was passed on the assumption that the 1929 Act would protect viable (and only viable) foetuses. Section 5(1) of the Abortion Act states that 'Nothing in this Act shall affect the provisions of the Infant Life (Preservation) Act 1929 (protecting the life of the viable foetus)' – the parenthesized phrase is in the original.

Section 1(2) of the Infant Life (Preservation) Act (1929) states: 'For the purposes of this Act, evidence that a woman had at any material time been pregnant for a period of twenty-eight weeks or more shall be prima facie proof that she was at that time pregnant of a child capable of being born alive.' This implies that the purpose of the Act was to protect the lives of viable foetuses and so it gives a clue as to what the phrase in section 1(1) means.

All this is merely to observe that the father's action was a long shot. The Act was not designed for his problem, which was a quarrel with the lax Abortion Act (1967).

Now what about the actual words, 'capable of being born alive'? Well, they could in everyday language be taken to cover a foetus from day one. Or they could be taken to mean only a viable foetus. But the legal techniques for interpreting such an ambiguous phrase require the judges to look at the Act as a whole, to construe the words in their context, with a sense of the purpose for which the Act was passed. I have endeavoured to do this and to show why it was wishful thinking for anti-abortionists to expect the courts to interpret 'capable of being born alive' as covering the foetus in question.

The judges unanimously chose breathing as the test and said that the affidavit evidence suggested that a foetus at this stage of development would not be able to breathe naturally or even with the aid of a respirator, because the lungs would be too immature. It follows that when the foetus is able to pass that test, say by 24 weeks, the offence of child destruction would be committed. So the presumption of 28 weeks, contained in section 1(2) of the Infant Life (Preservation) Act (1929) is not the last word and the true legal limit for abortions is 24 weeks or whenever the foetus is capable of breathing.

The Pavlovian reaction of criticizing the judges should therefore be resisted. Indeed, both counsel for the mother and for the father praised the judges for the manner in which they had handled the case. The litigation went through the High Court, Court of Appeal and on to the Appeal Committee of the House of Lords in record time. Mrs Justice Heilbron and the Court of Appeal were so certain and convincing that the Appeal Committee of the House of Lords saw no possibility of success in a full hearing.

The judges in the Court of Appeal decided at some speed. Then the parties rushed off to the Law Lords where the Appellate Committee decided not to hear full argument. The Court of Appeal thereafter declined to give further details of their reasons. Counsel for the father protested vigorously but made no impression on the Master of the Rolls. This has the disadvantage that we are left without the detailed account of the factors which the judges say influenced them. But there is little doubt in the minds of those who were in court (as I was) that beneath the analysis of the statutory language, lay the concern of Sir John Donaldson and his brethren that they should not upset the controversial border between legal and illegal abortions. They sensed the consequences of a change in the assumptions as to the law and they felt that any changes should be made by Parliament. Of that, I am sure. Nevertheless, their interpretation of the past law was itself convincing although anyone can see that this was by no means the only or even perhaps the most obvious interpretation.

Within a matter of weeks, however, another issue of law and morals did pass that last hurdle and the Law Lords gave leave for the Official Solicitor to appeal against a decision of the Court of Appeal to authorize the sterilization of a mentally handicapped seventeen-year-old girl. Whereas the abortion case turned on the interpretation of statutes, the sterilization decision allowed the judges more or less complete discretion.

In this latter case, therefore, the Law Lords considered a disturbing question: should a court authorize the sterilization of a mentally handicapped young woman? Some parents, doctors and social workers might believe that they themselves should be able to decide whether or not to sterilize a mentally handicapped teenager who is under their care. But the Court of Appeal and the House of Lords have both rightly rejected that view. To that extent, their judgments are to be welcomed as a tightening of the law and practice.

Yet all the judges who heard this case at all levels were prepared to authorize the sterilization of this particular seventeen-year-old. They said that they were acting in 'the best interests of the girl' as a matter of last resort.

At this point, several objections could be made. First, some critics believe that sterilization, or at least compulsory sterilization of those unable to give or refuse consent, is always unacceptable. Second, some believe that sterilization should only have been contemplated for therapeutic or medical reasons, and not merely as a form of contraception. Third, some would accept other forms of contraception but believe that the irreversible nature of sterilization makes it the wrong choice. Fourth, some accept the need for sterilization in some such cases but fear a drift down the path towards eugenics (a link which the judges strenuously denied) and bemoan the insensitive, demeaning discussion which lumps together people under labels such as 'the mentally handicapped'. Fifth, some critics regret the Law Lords' failure to specify the criteria implicit in their vague 'best interests' test and wish that their Lordships had examined the human rights at stake in greater detail. Sixth, some critics feel that the judges missed an opportunity to clarify the law's responsibilities towards the mentally handicapped in adult life, since the ruling was based on a statutory jurisdiction which ends at the age of eighteen. Seventh, some critics think that the real blame lies at Parliament's doors where legislators consistently duck sensitive moral dilemmas and leave the judges to resolve the ensuing mess. Finally, some people are disturbed by the facts of the particular case and in particular by the fact that the girl in question was sterilized only days before her eighteenth birthday, at which point the authority of this judgment would have expired. Professor Ian Kennedy and I raised many of these concerns in an article in *The Times* on the day before the Law Lords' hearing. That article was discussed in the course of counsel's argument but in the end the judges rejected any alternatives to the approach of the lower courts.

In contrast to the wide range of public concern, the Law Lords themselves had no doubts at all about their decision to authorize the sterilization. Lord Bridge, for example, claimed that,

> It is clear beyond argument that for her pregnancy would be an unmitigated disaster. The only question is how she may best be protected against it. The evidence proves overwhelmingly that the right answer is by a simple operation for occlusion of the Fallopian tubes . . . I find it difficult to understand how anybody examining the facts humanely, compassionately and objectively could reach any other conclusion.

But one might perhaps reach other conclusions for a variety of humane, compassionate and objective reasons. First, would pregnancy really be such a disaster? Second, if it would be disastrous, should she not be protected against sexual exploitation so that the question of pregnancy would never arise? Third, even if one was prepared to tolerate a contraceptive solution to her problems, is irreversible sterilization the right option?

On the first claim that pregnancy would be a disaster, Lord Oliver, for instance, says that, 'Should she become pregnant, it would be desirable that the pregnancy should be terminated.' But why? The baby would not be at risk. The mother, according to the specialist evidence, 'would tolerate the condition of pregnancy without undue distress'. Admittedly, she would have to be delivered by Caesarean section since she would panic unduly during normal childbirth. The Law Lords were worried that she would pick at the post-operative scar but that hardly seems a ground for an abortion, even within the present legislation!

On the second question of sexual experience, none of their Lordships takes the point that she ought to be protected against sexual exploitation whether or not she could become pregnant. They seem to be contrasting the fear of an unsterilized girl becoming pregnant causing her to lead a restricted life with the greater freedom that they would allow her once sterilized. Are these really the alternatives?

On the third point of choosing between various contraceptive measures, there is an argument that the irreversibility of sterilization makes it even less desirable and even more symbolically degrading. On the other hand, the Law Lords thought that, say, the contraceptive pill would involve a daily violation of the girl's privacy and would be far more risky as a contraceptive and would perhaps have harmful side-effects for a girl with her particular physical problems (such as epilepsy and obesity). That takes us back to the point that everybody in the case seems to have assumed that *some* form of contraception was inevitable and desirable.

What is most surprising, given the gravity of the issue and the widespread public concern, is that the judges seemed to gloss over all the difficult questions in their judgments. Their analysis of the past legal principle, the future consequences of their decision and their ability to have decided differently was unsatisfactory. But were there any signs of hope in the case? Yes, the public outcry at least forced the Law Lords to consider the matter and if the pressure is maintained, this might in turn lead on to our legislators considering a proper structure of rights and care for mentally handicapped people of whatever age and whatever mix of abilities and disabilities.

What is particularly intriguing for our purpose as students of judicial reasoning, however, is that another final court of appeal, the Canadian Supreme Court, had just examined the same question. In the case of *Re Eve*, it answered the same question with the opposite conclusion.

The Canadian court had three advantages over the Law Lords. First, it had time, perhaps too much in that it took sixteen months after the hearing for the Supreme Court to produce its judgment. The Law Lords decided after only one day's argument on 2 April and gave their judgments three weeks later. The rush was because everyone in the British case assumed, perhaps wrongly, that if the girl were not sterilized before her eighteenth birthday on 20 May, nobody, not even the court, would thereafter have been able to authorize treatment for her since statute decreed that she would then cease to be a ward of court.

The second advantage was that there were several *amici curiae* presenting the views of interested third parties to the Canadian court so that it could benefit from the widest range of arguments in evaluating the consequences of alternative decisions.

The third helpful factor was that the Supreme Court was also able to rely, for this task, on the research of the Canadian Law Commission. The Law Commissions here, however, have consistently failed to address questions of medical law and ethics. Parliament fails to reform the law to keep pace with medical developments and the challenges they pose. The courts meanwhile are left to solve issues of the greatest moral import, often in a rush and without the benefit of considered reflection of public policy. This has happened with teenage contraception and with abortion, it is happening with surrogacy and it may well happen with AIDS. The time for a better method is overdue. The long-term solution might be to follow the US, the French and others by creating a Commission on Medical Law and Ethics.

La Forest J, giving judgment for all nine members of the Supreme Court in *Re Eve*, concluded that,

> The grave intrusion on a person's rights and the certain physical damage that ensues from non-therapeutic sterilization without consent, when compared to the highly questionable advantage that can result from it, have persuaded me that it can never safely be determined that such a procedure is for the benefit of that person. Accordingly, the procedure

should never be authorized for non-therapeutic purposes under the *parens patriae* jurisdiction.

The court agreed that sterilization may, on occasion, be necessary and lawful as 'treatment of a serious malady'. The crucial distinction is between sterilization for medical reasons (therapeutic sterilization), which may be permissible, and sterilization for non-medical reasons such as for contraception, which was absolutely unacceptable to the Supreme Court.

The Law Lords were not, of course, bound to follow the Canadian Supreme Court. They are not even bound to follow themselves, let alone a court in another jurisdiction. But once the case had been drawn to their attention (and the case was not cited to the lower courts in *Re B* – it was only when the Court of Appeal's decision became headline news that academics pointed out the significance of the Canadian judgment), the Law Lords were prepared to consider it.

As I have said, they were also prepared to consider an article in the previous day's *Times*, written by Ian Kennedy and myself. The judges were distinctly unimpressed by the headline of that article: 'This rush to judgment'. It was an unusual experience to sit in court watching the Law Lords rustle their newspapers and hearing them refer to the 'paragraph to the right of the picture'. We have at least come some way since my student days a decade ago, when some judges still claimed that the only good academic was a dead academic. They may still *think* that, but they have abandoned the old idea that only old textbooks can be cited in court. Yesterday's newspapers are now acceptable.

Professor Kennedy and I suggested that there were four possible approaches which the Law Lords could have adopted. The first would have been to defer to the girl's mother, guardians and doctors. Some claim that this has been the practice in this country. But Heilbron J rightly rejected that argument in a case decided ten years ago. The question is not one of solely clinical judgement sinnce it involves issues of human rights which transcend the competence of doctors.

The second approach was better, and the one which in effect the Law Lords adopted, but it was still unsatisfactory. This is the 'last resort' test adopted by the Court of Appeal. This has the advantages of removing the decision to a disinterested authority, the court, and of emphasizing that sterilization is only to be considered *in extremis*. But 'last resort' needs defining, otherwise it could slip back into the first approach of what doctors deem to be the last resort.

The third method would have been that of the Canadian provincial court in *Eve*. The 'best interests' and 'last resort' tests are spelt out in detail. Sterilization would only be available if a series of fourteen difficult steps are taken. The onus is very firmly on those who are arguing for sterilization to show that it is the only solution to a real problem. They must show, for instance, that the real object of the operation is to protect the girl not her parents or other carers; that other forms of contraception would be unworkable; that there is a real danger, rather than a mere chance, of pregnancy; and that there is more compelling evidence than the mere existence of a handicap that pregnancy would have a damaging effect. On reflection, my personal view is that this is the most attractive path.

The fourth approach would have been that of the Supreme Court. Even if all the provincial court's fourteen hurdles could be surmounted, the Canadian Supreme Court would still not permit sterilization because, as Lord Eldon said, under the *parens patriae* jurisdiction, 'it has always been the principle of this Court, not to risk damage to children which it cannot repair'. The irreversible nature of sterilization means that although the fourteen steps might lead a court towards, say, long-term contraceptive injections for a mentally handicapped girl, they could never justify the final step of sterilization, unless the operation was needed for medical reasons. Why? As the Canadian Law Commission observed, 'sterilized mentally retarded persons tend to perceive sterilization as a symbol of reduced or degraded status. Their attempts to pass for normal were hindered by negative self-perceptions and resulted in withdrawal and isolation.' The Supreme Court would reject exceptions beyond the therapeutic proviso by saying no, find another way, do not use irreversible surgery to solve social problems, the danger to human rights is too great. The Law Lords rejected this approach, finding the distinction between therapeutic and non-therapeutic elusive or unhelpful.

Personally, I find the Law Lords' judgments elusive and unhelpful. In my opinion, they failed to tackle the difficult questions raised by the case and failed to offer sufficiently detailed guidance so as to assist future dilemmas which involve mentally handicapped young women.

By now, you will appreciate, we have gone beyond worrying about the reaction of Dworkin or Griffith. Perhaps the Canadian decision and the British one can both be explained as quests for (reversible ?) principles. Perhaps the background of the Canadian judges is different in a way which accounts for the disagreement. But what is far more important is that the British judges' analysis of my second and third factors seems superficial when compared to the careful approach of the Canadian Supreme Court. This is important because it affects the lives of thousands of people.

I am not here disputing the result in the *Re B* so much as the analysis, or the lack thereof. The conclusion of the case does not solve Jeanette's problems. Sterilization does not absolve those with responsibility for her from using their best endeavours to protect her from sexual exploitation. Nor does the case solve the problems of other young women like Jeanette. Nor should judges have been expected to solve all these problems. As the Supreme Court itself acknowledged in Eve's case:

> Judges are generally ill-informed about many of the factors relevant to a wise decision in this area. They generally know little of mental illness, of techniques of contraception or their efficacy. And, however well presented a case may be, it can only partially inform. If sterilization of the mentally incompetent is to be adopted as desirable for general social purposes, the legislature is the appropriate body to do so. It is in a position to inform itself and it is attuned to the feelings of the public in making policy in this sensitive area.

This is a statement of brutal honesty which deserves our attention when we consider the role of judges as law-makers. There are limits to their competence and legitimacy.

Hence the wider significance of the *Re B* argument was that public attention was drawn to yet another problem of medical law and ethics where Parliament has failed to guide the judges. In future, Parliament should take on these dilemmas of modern medicine. And as a first step, it should set up an appropriate body to review the problems and put the arguments before the nation. Although our judges deploy their considerable concern and ability when confronted by these questions under adverse conditions, the present British piecemeal approach to such fundamental problems is inadequate. Issues of human rights deserve more than their day in court.

The sterilization case also raised a couple of wider issues of relevance to our concern in judging judges. First, why do we have a two-tier system of appeals? What is the role of the Law Lords? We do not really need two sets of appellate judges to rehearse the facts. Yet that is more or less all they did in *Re B*. The Law Lords declined to take the opportunity to decide the *parens patriae* point, whether there is an inherent jurisdiction to care for those who cannot care for themselves which survives the age limit of eighteen which terminates the statutory wardship jurisdiction. They declined the opportunity to give more guidance than is provided by simply incanting the phrase 'best interests'.

Not only does this case therefore raise questions about the role of the full Judicial Committee, it also reminds us of the role of the Appeal Committee of the House of Lords which had by 1987 grown accustomed to convening at great speed to decide whether to grant leave in cases of great public interest. The Law Lords' willingness to consider the granting of leave in such circumstances is to be applauded. But observers may be unsure of the criteria by which they decide when to grant and when to refuse leave. In *C v. S* (the abortion case discussed above), the Committee refused leave to appeal. In *Re B*, however, leave was granted. Since the Law Lords in the sterilization judgment clearly did not find any difficulty at all in resolving the point of law, it might seem that it was the public clamour which weighed heavily with the Appeal Committee, and perhaps the cumulative clamour building on dissatisfaction in some quarters with both Court of Appeal decisions. It seems that the Law Lords were really taking the opportunity to explain the facts which they felt justified the Court of Appeal decision, which had been subjected to so much criticism.

The Law Lords' judgments in *Re B* gave the impression that the general principle enunciated by the courts below was blindingly obvious and that the outcome turned on the facts. Yet they wanted very much to restate the Court of Appeal's judgment authoritatively in the face of public criticism. How this squares with the role of the second-tier appeal deserves deeper examination.

The second point of practice which arises from the Law Lords' hearing is the unsatisfactory treatment accorded to the European Convention on Human Rights in the course of oral argument. The Law Lords seemed happy enough to be referred to the Convention. But they were not referred to the relevant Articles and the interpretation of the Article which was cited left something to be desired. Counsel for the Official Solicitor, representing the child's interests, did not refer to the Convention, nor did counsel for the mother. But counsel for the local authority mentioned Article 12 in order to rebut the argument that the girl in question had a right to procreate. Article 12 is not the most conspicuous success story within the Convention. It runs as follows: 'Men and women of marriageable age have the right to marry and to found a family, subject to the national laws governing the exercise of this right.' That may not say much but it perhaps says more than counsel supposed. She argued that since the girl in this case did not have the capacity to consent to marriage she did not come within the terms of the Article and thus did not qualify for the right to found a family. Others might suppose that the European Convention would not be interpreted by its own institutions so as to allow the right to procreate only to married couples. And they would suspect that there must be more relevant Articles elsewhere in the Convention. They would be right. Article 8 on the right to respect for one's private and family life, Article 3 prohibiting inhuman or degrading treatment, and even Article 2's right to life ought to have been considered. Even if the right rights had been pinpointed, some idea of the jurisprudence and interpretive approach of the European Court of Human Rights should surely have been forthcoming. Of course, counsel and the court were arguing at short notice but if the Law Lords really are determining questions of law of general public importance, the principles of human rights law deserve more careful attention. Sure enough, our next case displays more concern for the human rights dimensions of the law.

15

Spycatcher

———

Once upon a time, spies spied and reporters reported. All that changed in the summer of 1987. The former spy, Peter Wright, had turned reporter, writing about his days in MI5 and publishing abroad a bestselling book, *Spycatcher*. Some reporters also seemed to switch professions. The *Sunday Times* mounted a huge undercover operation in July 1987, involving decoys and dummy editions, to print extracts from *Spycatcher* before the Attorney-General could get wind of their intentions and seek an injunction to stop publication.

Spies and reporters joined together in judging judges when the matter did come to court. And it has come to court time and time again in one country after another. In the UK, there will eventually be at least three decisions of the House of Lords on *Spycatcher*. *Spycatcher* I is the decision to grant an interim injunction against some newspapers from repeating Wright's allegations before the full trial of the dispute between the newspapers and the Government. *Spycatcher* II will be the decision as to whether the interim injunctions against certain named newspapers are also binding on all other journalists. *Spycatcher* III will be the appeal from the full trial itself.

In many ways, it is *Spycatcher* II which will have the greatest ramifications for the media and the law. And it is *Spycatcher* III which will be decisive over the future coverage of Wright's allegations in the British press. But it was *Spycatcher* I which first captured the public's attention. *Spycatcher* I was a decision which led to unprecedented criticism of the judiciary from the British press (not surprisingly, since they lost), from commentators around the world where legal systems had allowed publication of Wright's allegations, and even from within the British judiciary itself. I shall therefore focus on the story of *Spycatcher* I in this chapter. All other references to '*Spycatcher*' or 'the case' should be taken as referring to *Spycatcher* I unless the contrary is stated. There is another reason for not concentrating on II or III. As I write, they have not yet been decided although I expect the results to be known before this book is published. I am torn between the desire to show how to predict the results of cases and the caution imposed by my own strictures in this chapter and elsewhere that commentators should not rush in to criticize before they have read the full reasons of the judges, let alone before the case has even started.

I should also warn the reader that whereas my views on the proper outcome in most cases probably coincide with at least one of Dworkin or Griffith and with many other academics, my approach to *Spycatcher* seems unpopular. From the start, I maintained that the proper outcome to the interim decision would be to preserve the position of the parties until the full trial, at which point I would expect the press to win. In other words, I maintain that there is considerable legal sense in the judges deciding that the press should lose phase I but win phase III. This is unpopular with the press because they obviously think that they should win all the time and newspapers have a special interest in running stories as soon as possible. Moreover, *interim* injunctions have often been decisive, as we have seen in the earlier chapter on the miners' strike and as we shall see in a later chapter when we look briefly at other litigation between the Attorney-General and the *Sunday Times*.

The legal niceties of distinguishing between interim and final injunctions have often been lost in the welter of criticism of the judges over *Spycatcher*. I should just explain, therefore, that it does take time to organize a full trial of a legal dispute. Innumerable documents have to be assembled and assimilated by the lawyers. Busy lawyers on all sides and very busy and important witnesses such as Sir Robert (now Lord) Armstrong, the former Cabinet Secretary, have to find a common space in their diaries for a trial which can last weeks, and the courts have a backlog of cases which makes the finding of court time difficult. So there is often a swift hearing before a judge but without the witnesses and without the detailed argument which will follow. The judge then decides what to do pending the full trial. Where one side is eager to publish something which the other side claims is confidential and prejudicial to national security, then the former is going to try to convince the judge at the interim stage that there is nothing of substance in the latter's argument. And it would indeed be a grave impediment to an investigative press if injunctions could succeed against them at the interim stage on flimsy grounds. That would allow unmeritorious litigants effectively to gag the press because, by the time the full trial proceeded, there might be little news value left in the story. But if there is genuinely an arguable claim that publication would be in breach of confidence or a threat to national security, then the consequences of refusing an interim injunction could be deleterious. A judge might well be tempted to err on the side of safety. At best, he would have preserved the secrecy of information which a full trial might suggest needs protection. At worst, he would only have delayed the press. The resulting injunction, if any, is described variously as interlocutory, temporary or interim.

I should stress that the obvious solution to the difficulties faced by all sides over *Spycatcher* is to speed up the process by which cases come to full trial. That concern is being addressed in the wake of the Civil Justice Review.

Above all, I should make clear that I regard the Government's attempts to restrain the moderate reporting by the British press of Peter Wright's allegations as misguided and counter-productive. But that is not the issue which faced the judges. They were not asked whether the Government was tactically wise to stand on its legal rights nor even, in *Spycatcher* I whether the Government had any legal rights on which to stand but whether they should allow the Government to remain standing until its legal claims could be fully analysed in a court and its witnesses cross-examined.

The conclusion reached by a majority of the Law Lords in *Spycatcher* I was that an interim injunction should be granted. The Law Lords had once again moved very quickly to hear the case at a week's notice. Given the apparent urgency of, and interest in, the case, they took the unusual step of announcing their result the following week with the promise to give the full reasons for their decision later. The issue was whether to grant the Government a temporary injunction to ban newspapers from repeating allegations contained in a book which was not yet published in the UK, but which was widely available elsewhere, the foreign copies of which could be brought into the UK by private individuals.

By a 3–2 majority, the Law Lords granted the injunction in terms that were even broader than those asked for by the Government. The press were outraged. The *Daily Mirror*, for example, ran a banner headline the next day, accompanied by upside-down photographs of the majority Law Lords, which left its readers in no doubt of the paper's estimation of the judges: 'You Fools!'

But the first error in this kind of judging of the judges is to rush to judgment without waiting to read the judges' reasoning. Even in more sedate surroundings, that is to say, the letters columns of *The Times*, others joined in the attack on the majority judges. To my surprise, Lord Scarman wrote a letter to *The Times* on 3 August 1987 taking the majority to task in advance of the detailed judgments. Why was this surprising? Well, Lord Scarman himself had made the point against such premature criticism in an earlier letter to *The Times* on 31 July 1980, when he defended his colleagues in the *British Steel v. Granada* case who were similarly attacked. He then expressed sadness and anger at the rush to judge the judges when 'All that is known of the decision is that the Lords have dismissed the appeal. Neither the reasons for the decision nor its true scope will be known until the members of the appellate committee deliver their speeches. It would have served the nation better if you had forborne from a sweeping condemnation of the judiciary based, largely, on the decision until its true nature and limits were made known.' This must be the fundamental rule in judging judges, at least for those of us who believe that the law does and should involve reasoning. If anyone really believes the Nightmare, I suppose, they need not wait until the reasons are given but could merely look up the judges' education and 'explain' the decision on those grounds.

Stung by the ill-informed criticism, the Law Lords brought forward the announcement of their reasons. Those who bothered to read the full judgments, conveniently and laudably printed in full by *The Times*, would have discovered that the majority Law Lords were not as asinine as the media had declared them to be.

Their judgments made sense. Given that the Law Lords were only being asked to preserve the status quo until the full trial, the decision was not unreasonable.

But publication of their judgments added to, rather than quelled, the hostility towards the majority Law Lords. Indeed, the majority judges were no longer being attacked solely from the serried ranks of the press but also from within the Judicial Committee itself. One of the dissenting Law Lords, Lord Bridge, launched a vigorous denunciation of the majority, observing that 'freedom of speech is always the first casualty under a totalitarian regime' and claiming that the *Spycatcher* saga was now taking a 'significant step down that very dangerous road'. The Government would, he claimed, face 'inevitable condemnation and humiliation by the European Court of Human Rights in Strasbourg'.

That is just where he is wrong, according to the majority. Lord Ackner saw 'no prospect of the Convention availing' the press. Lord Templeman based his judgment precisely on attempting to anticipate how the European Court of Human Rights would decide the matter, examining Article 10 and applying it closely.

All the judges seemed to agree on one thing, however, namely that strong language was appropriate. The majority joined in the vituperation. Lord Brandon said that to have decided otherwise would have been 'anarchic'. Lord Ackner castigated the press without reservation, talked of 'press hysteria', an abuse of power and a depressing reflection of falling standards, and asked whether the critics would like the law to become a jellyfish rather than a rock.

Lord Ackner said that the cry for a sense of proportion went 'totally unheeded by the entire media'. He asked for but a 'tithe' of the publicity given to the ill-informed criticisms to be accorded to the basis and the reasons given. He even offered to help readers understand the judgment by lots of underlining for emphasis and, no doubt, for leader-writers.

The majority all stressed that it was an interim injunction, preserving the position until the full trial. Wright's allegations relate to events of twelve years ago, therefore why the rush to publish today when the full trial will give a definitive answer tomorrow? The response might be well, when is the full trial going to happen? A good point, but the majority did urge all speed in the holding of the full trial.

Next the majority emphasized that the press's argument that the book was available via the USA was not decisive. If availability and knowledge by the British public were the same thing, why would everyone be so eager to publish stale news?

Then the majority showed that just because the confidentiality argument looks thin now that the confidences have been breached by publication abroad, this does not exhaust the full force of the argument. There might be further public interests in setting examples so as to discourage other former spies from publishing their memoirs and perhaps damaging national security.

Lord Templeman was very careful to emphasize that he was deciding in a democratic framework, that Article 10 of the European Convention which declares a right of freedom of expression, including a right to a free press, accepts restrictions on free speech if they are 'necessary' in the interests of, for example, national security, the protection of information received in confidence, and to maintain the authority and impartiality of the judiciary. He went to some lengths to show that an interim injunction in these circumstances was 'necessary'.

Lord Oliver dissented with 'a degree of hesitation', finding the case

> uniquely difficult because of the cogency of the arguments on both sides and of the very finely balanced considerations which, partly as a matter of convenience and partly as a matter of policy, require to be taken into account. There was a point during the argument when the skill of Mr Mummery's advocacy almost persuaded me to take the same view as the majority of your Lordships. Further reflection impelled me to an opposite conclusion, but I mention it lest, in the predictable clamour aroused when your Lordships' decision was announced, it should be thought that the solution of the very difficult problem came easily or obviously to any member of your Lordships' House.

Lord Oliver's major grievance with the majority was that they had overturned a careful first-instance judgment by the Vice-Chancellor, Sir Nicolas Browne-Wilkinson, whereas they should have respected his view even if they would have differed, unless he was unreasonably wrong. He disagreed on the role of an appellate judge. The Law Lords should not act as if they were the first-instance judge but only intervene when that judge has erred substantially. Since the case was so finely balanced, Lord Oliver would have left intact the Vice Chancellor's decision to lift the injunctions.

Lord Bridge really seemed to take issue with the majority on the consequences of their decision in the real world, that is to say, he believed that the ban would look more and more ridiculous and felt that the anomaly of availability but not publication should be ended immediately.

Although Lord Brandon was especially clear in looking at both the legal principle *and* the social consequences, one hallmark of this case was that *all* the Law Lords were fully aware of the threefold influences on their decision. They could hardly be otherwise when the attention of the nation's press was upon them. The media discussion hardly mentioned the first factor, the law on confidentiality and national security, but focused on the consequentialist strain of thought and the question of the role of the judges in a democracy. The judges responded in kind without overmuch analysis of the British precedents.

But the other distinguishing feature of the case is the irony it contains for the Bill of Rights argument. Predictably enough, the Bill of Rights lobby fastened on the *Spycatcher* decision as illustrating the need for a domestic Bill of Rights. Indeed, that was the thrust of Lord Scarman's letter to *The Times*. The argument, you will remember, seems to be that we cannot trust the judges to protect our civil liberties, so we need to incorporate the European Convention on Human Rights into British law. But the proponents of the Bill of Rights idea shot themselves in the foot by their premature rejoicing. For when the reasons were published, it emerged that Lord Templeman, giving the major judgment for the majority, based his entire argument on the premise that we already had a Bill of Rights, that Article 10 of the European Convention was already the controlling feature of the past law which he had to interpret. Although Lord Bridge asserted that the case would be reversed by the European Court, it was Lord Templeman who went through the relevant Article line by line and who performed the balancing act which it requires between the right to freedom of expression and its numerous exceptions. Thus the fascinating feature of the case for our purposes is that the *Spycatcher* majority decided as if we already had the very thing their opponents claim we need to stop them deciding in the way which they did!

Of course, the Billophiles can justifiably claim that the case has shown they have won their campaign, that we already have a Bill of Rights, even if it does not show that this will resolve all the problems of judging judges. But I myself suspect that Lord Templeman would have been less willing to place so much emphasis on the European Convention if he had not realized that any judge could have used the broad provisions of Article 10 to justify any result in more or less any case on freedom of expression. I personally think that the case for a Bill of Rights is far from proven unless and until more attention is paid to the key questions of who is going to interpret it and how they are going to do so. Those are the concerns of this book.

We will indeed return to the Bill of Rights argument later, as well as my broader concerns that the more important points are to do with the choice of interpreters and their approach to judicial decision-making rather than with the status of the text to be interpreted. But this is an opportune time to ask *why* did Lord Templeman and the other judges refer to the European Convention on Human Rights? The answer is that they were responding to counsels' arguments. And this is in itself of great importance. It shows that new approaches to judging can be accommodated by the British judiciary if only barristers put new arguments to the judges. That is why, in the suggestions for further reading at the end of this book, I urge law students always to read counsels' arguments in the official law reports. That is why I am confident that the hitherto clandestine second and third factors which I claim are inherent in judicial resolution of hard cases – the evaluation of the consequences and the consideration of the judges' own role – will eventually be much more openly and readily acknowledged and argued about in the courts.

As far as the European Convention is concerned, Anthony Lester QC deserves much of the credit for raising its provisions in argument before British judges. He appeared in *Spycatcher* for the

Sunday Times, together with his junior colleague, David Pannick. I have teased this pair in print before, referring to them as the Batman and Robin of our legal system, an intrepid duo of caped crusaders who put the world to writs. I do not share their apparent confidence that a Bill of Rights is the answer to our problems of civil liberties. But I have also praised their legal talents. Indeed, I have predicted that David Pannick will become the outstanding judge of the next century. For present purposes, what is important is that barristers can change the thrust of their presentation and succeed thereby in changing the orientation of the judges' opinions. If Lester and Pannick can persuade the courts to look towards Europe, then they and other innovative barristers can also persuade the judges to discuss other important aids to good decision-making such as an open analysis of the consequences of their decisions.

When the full trial took place, Lester and Pannick were able to persuade Mr Justice Scott to go further than Lord Templeman had done, although not perhaps far enough for their particular client, the *Sunday Times*. If the first stage was Lord Templeman's textual analysis of Article 10, the second phase was the trial judge's readiness to look in detail at the decisions of the European Court of Human Rights which interpreted that provision. This helped convince the judge that the Government's case did not stand up on full examination. On 22 December 1987, he gave his judgment in *Spycatcher* III. Not only his reading of the European and British legal material but also the changed reality of world-wide distribution and the unimpressive evidence for the Government as to how there might be any further threat to national security from responsible newspaper coverage by the *Guardian* and the *Observer* all contributed to Mr Justice Scott's conclusion that the interim injunctions against the papers should be lifted. He was less impressed by the *Sunday Times* which had begun to serialize the Wright book (whereas the *Observer* and the *Guardian* were originally, back in 1986, just reporting the then imminent Australian court proceedings and taking the opportunity to summarize Wright's allegations). But the press had begun to win. The press stopped lambasting the judiciary. A Daniel had come to judgment. Incidentally, this Daniel has already appeared in an earlier chapter. Those who preferred the

Griffithesque view of the miners' strike case to the Dworkinian interpretation, should note that this is the same Mr Justice Scott. If his decision in the earlier case is regarded as sympathetic to the Government (which was not, of course, a party to that intra-class dispute), at least his decision in this case cannot be similarly dismissed.

Then three Daniels came along to confirm Mr Justice Scott's decision in the Court of Appeal on 10 February 1988. There were some disagreements among the appellate judges, particularly with regard to the *Sunday Times*. One judge, Lord Justice Bingham, thought that that paper should succeed as had the other papers, and that it was not legally in the wrong in publishing the serialization. But even he had reservations about the way in which the reporters had turned to the methods of the spies, describing the editor's behaviour in launching the serialization as 'devious and surreptitious'. The Court of Appeal again mixed analysis of the past law with what one suspects was a healthy concern for the consequences of their decision in the real world. As Lord Justice Dillon put it, 'for the courts to continue the injunctions further would be futile and just plain silly, now that *Spycatcher* has been so widely circulated'. And the Master of the Rolls, Lord Donaldson observed that 'Justice was only blind or blindfolded to the extent necessary to hold its scales evenly. It was not, and must never be allowed to become, blind to the realities of the situation, lamentable though the situation might be.'

It is not appropriate for me now to analyse the decisions in *Spycatcher* III any further, for various reasons. First, I would be in danger of ignoring my own injunction to wait for the full versions of the judgments before venturing criticism, since I am writing this as the judgments have just been handed down. They are not yet available in the law reports in full. Second, this chapter has been primarily concerned with *Spycatcher* I. I am just pleased that *Spycatcher* III is, thus far, bearing out my sense of how the case ought to proceed. Third, in between my writing this and you reading it, we will have witnessed the Law Lords' resolution of *Spycatcher* III in the summer of 1988. I suspect that the Government will put up a better argument before the Law Lords. The next phase beyond referring to the European Convention cases on Article 10, for example, would be for the Government to point out that the cases hitherto cited to the courts have not been ones where the 'national security' exception has been invoked. Where the European Court has been presented with that exception (which exists for several other articles in the Convention), that Court has been most reluctant to reject it. If the Government does indeed run that line of argument, it would have a hint of Dworkinian integrity about it, trying to analogize from other parts of the law. But I still suspect that, at the end of the day, the absurd consequences of a permanent injunction will be decisive.

Whatever the outcome of *Spycatcher* III, it seems difficult to believe that the judging of judges by the press can reach such vituperative proportions as it did in the previous summer. But what remains surprising to many people about *Spycatcher* I is the way in which the *judges* criticized one another. Yet the level of mutual recrimination in the *Spycatcher* judgments is not unprecedented. Judges have occasionally accused one another of living in Wonderland, of Humptydumptyism, of definition by fiat. But is it unfortunate? Not necessarily – it gives the lie to the fairy tale that the common law is like an Aladdin's cave with a judge having only to say Open Sesame for the decision to emerge. Law is not like that at the higher levels of the courts. The law is uncertain. Judges are engaged in defining, refining, developing, making law. They can disagree just like politicians. So, this sharpness has the merit of exposing that truth. But we expect judges to give reasoned explanations for their value judgements and to do so only after reflecting on all and only the arguments presented to them. Because we do not have the sanction of removing them from office, we need the dialogue between judges and judged. Otherwise Lord Hailsham's *bête noire*, the elective dictatorship, will be supplanted by an even worse problem, the unelective dictatorship.

Part III

Judges

———

Great Judges

———

American jurists are fascinated with the idea of the great judge. They compile lists of what constitutes greatness in a judge and of who best matches the criteria. Thus Professor Abraham suggests we look for these qualities:

1 demonstrated judicial temperament
2 professional expertise and competence
3 absolute personal as well as professional integrity
4 an able, agile, lucid mind
5 appropriate professional educational background or training
6 the ability to communicate clearly, both orally and in writing, especially the latter.

Professor Goldman has a similar list:

1 neutrality as to the parties in litigation
2 fair-mindedness
3 being well versed in the law
4 ability to think and write logically and lucidly
5 personal integrity
6 good physical and mental health
7 judicial temperament
8 ability to handle judicial power sensibly.

Sadly, these are not quite the criteria by which Supreme Court Justices are appointed. We shall explore this later when we look at the unsuccessful nomination of Robert Bork to the Supreme Court in 1987. It seems that the Justices' nominations turn on:

1 objective merit
2 personal friendship

3 balancing representation or representativeness on the court
4 real political and ideological compatibility.

Only the first of these would coincide with the professorial lists. Talking of which, the professors proceed to issue questionnaires to fellow 'court-watchers'. Hence 65 academic observers were asked to grade the judges in 1970: 12 greats, 15 near-greats, 55 average, 6 below average and 8 failures emerged. Chief Justice Marshall got all 65 votes as great, Brandeis 62, Holmes 61, Black 42. The other 8 greats, in chronological order, were Story, Taney, Harlan I, Hughes, Stone, Cardozo, Frankfurter and Warren.

The organizers of the survey deduced that greatness resulted from a combination of the following qualities:

1 scholarship
2 legal learning and analytical powers
3 craftsmanship and technique
4 wide general knowledge and learning
5 character, moral integrity and impartiality
6 diligence and industry
7 the ability to express oneself orally with clarity, logic and compelling force
8 openness to change
9 courage to take unpopular decisions
10 dedication to the court as an institution and to the office of Supreme Court Justice
11 ability to carry a proportionate share of the court's responsibility in opinion-writing, and finally
12 the quality of statesmanship.

With the outstanding exception of Alan Paterson's study, *The Law Lords*, the UK has not emulated the American interest in great judges. There have been very few biographies of twentieth-century judges. Geoffrey Lewis's life of Lord Atkin and Professor Heuston's *Lives of the Lord Chancellors* are exceptions. The editors of a collection of essays on Lord Denning have called for legal scholarship to examine the record of judges like Lords Reid, Diplock and Wilberforce.

The editor of another collection of essays, this time a tribute to Griffith, has called for British scholars to practise the American art of jurimetrics, of quantitative analysis to complement the qualitative analysis. Who votes with whom, who was the greatest (in the sense of the most frequent) dissenter, who sided most often with the government, who decided against trade unions, and so on. We know the answers to some of these questions and I agree that we ought to be investigating them all.

Time is limited, however, and before we engage in those invaluable tasks, perhaps we should return to the qualitative questions of the right framework within which to investigate. Carol Harlow, Griffith's brilliant protégée and the aforesaid editor of his tribute, defends her hero against Paterson by claiming that Paterson's work is 'anecdotal' rather than, 'scientific'. In the end, she concludes, Paterson's findings are as 'impressionistic as Griffith who deliberately sets out to popularise and simplify'.

My own view is that we are all offering images of the cathedral of law and that Paterson's work, which took a dozen years from the beginning of his research to its publication, offers one of the most well-rounded portraits. But I can assure Carol Harlow and others that when I produce biographies of such legal luminaries as Lord Scarman, I shall include all manner of tables and statistics. For the present, however, I shall paint an impressionistic sketch which might, in its own way, reveal a little of the subject. I have chosen five judges for these purposes. My choice was constrained by various factors. First, Lords Denning, Devlin, Hailsham and Scarman are retired. Their judicial record is more or less complete, their jurisprudence more or less developed. It seems fairer to pick on them than on someone whose reputation is in transition. Second, they are the most well-known judges, media stars. Lords Reid, Diplock and Wilberforce were probably 'better' judges but many readers of this book will probably never have heard of the great Lord Reid, at most know of the brilliant Lord Wilberforce that his pro-miners (eat your heart out, Griffith) report helped bring down the Heath Government, and associate the intellectual but acerbic Lord Diplock with the eponymous Diplock courts. Third, my chosen judges represent a variety of attributes within the legal profession, they are all famous for something: Lord Denning as the judicial iconoclast; Lord Devlin as the judicial philosopher; Lord Hailsham as the politician and conservative; Lord Scarman as the liberal and professional inquiry chairman. My fifth judge is Lord Mackay of Clashfern, the new Lord Chancellor. Although it is to be hoped that he continues to sit as a judge, his appointment to the Woolsack is something of a watershed. He also promises to remain in the job for as long as Lord Hailsham did. His judicial style will exert enormous influence.

I shall sketch these five from different perspectives. This is not a competition to find the greatest judge. It is rather an attempt to give you the flavour of how our judges think, of who they are and what they do. I shall therefore focus on different aspects of the judicial personality in the different profiles. I shall judge Lord Devlin as an academic writer, Lord Hailsham as a colourful politician, Lord Mackay as a working judge converted into a politician, Lord Scarman as a jack of all judicial trades and master of most, and Lord Denning as, well, as Lord Denning.

Lord Denning

———

Unusually for a judge, Lord Denning has had several books written about his judicial career. He wrote most of them himself. He was a judicial iconoclast. He wrote in short sentences. Like this. He was not afraid to dissent. He was not afraid to develop the law. He preferred his version of justice to precedent. He was a judge for a very long time. He was a very influential judge as Master of the Rolls. Was he a great judge?

Well, his staccato prose style left something to be desired but the real questions concern his sense of justice and his propensity to superimpose it upon the law. In the cases which we have examined in some detail, Lord Denning was involved in the Fares Fair case and the Sikh boy case, but he really belongs to an earlier era.

Lord Denning was not prone to respect our first ingredient – past law. He prided himself on his robust approach to precedent:

> I would treat it as you would a path along the woods. You must follow it certainly so as to reach your end. But you must not let the path become too overgrown. You must cut out the dead wood and trim off the side branches else you will find yourself lost in thickets and brambles. My plan is simply to keep the path to justice clear of obstructions which would impede it. (*The Discipline of the Law*)

Perhaps this explains why Lord Denning was often accused of not seeing the wood for the trees. In more straightforward language, he put the same point thus:

> My root belief is that the proper role of the judge is to do justice between the parties before him. If there is any rule of law which impairs the doing of justice, then it is the province

of the judge to do all that he legitimately can to avoid the rule – or even to change it – so as to do justice in the instant case before him. He need not wait for legislation to intervene: because that can never be of any help in the instant case. I would emphasize, however, the word 'legitimately': the judge is himself subject to the law and must abide by it.

That last cautionary phrase does not seem to mean very much in the light of the preceding passage.

So how did Lord Denning discern and assess our second factor – social consequences? He had no doubts about what was just and unjust but these thoughts have often been described as lacking consistency. He thinks of himself as the champion of the little against the great, the weak against the powerful. He supported deserted wives against deserting husbands and the consumer against the businessman, but not the trade unions against employers, students against education authorities, aliens against the Home Office. So perhaps his self-image as a champion of the underdog is not an accurate picture.

Whence came his odd assortment of ideas? Was he a stereotype public schoolboy? Lord Denning's background has been well documented, by Lord Denning. He came from an extraordinarily talented family, including two brothers who became a lieutenant-general and a vice-admiral respectively. But the family were not rich and Tom Denning was given a free place at Andover Grammar School. He then won a scholarship to Magdalen College Oxford in 1916. Conscription interrupted his studies, but after service on the Western Front he returned to study for a First Class Honours degree in Mathematics. He taught for a year at Winchester but then won another scholarship which allowed him to return to Magdalen and take, within a year, a First in Jurisprudence. The President of Magdalen sent him a note: 'You are a marked man. Perhaps you will be a Lord of Appeal one day.' He was.

He was unsuccessful in the All Souls examination but went on to the Bar and survived, no mean feat for a young man without a private income in those times. He took silk just before the Second World War in which he served as legal adviser to the Regional Commissioner for the North-East. In 1944 he was appointed a judge, one of three silks elevated to cope with the anticipated flood of post-war divorces. He was young, forty-five, although not, as he has claimed, the youngest judge for 150 years. After eighteen months he was transferred to the King's Bench Division, a period best known to students for his judgment in the High Trees case. Then he became Judge for Pensions Appeals. Three years later he was promoted to the Court of Appeal. He was sometimes in trouble with the House of Lords and especially Viscount Simonds. But he was nevertheless promoted to the House of Lords in 1957. Five years later, he returned to the Court of Appeal as Master of the Rolls: 'Some would say that I moved down.' But he was shrewd enough to know better. Few cases go to the House of Lords and if they do, it is of little use to dissent. But in the Court of Appeal Lord Denning could handle many more cases, choose his colleagues and leave a real mark on the law. Even when he was in a minority, he might be able to trail a path for the litigant to take an appeal to the House of Lords and perhaps move the law in what Lord Denning regarded as the right direction.

Lord Scarman has described the next two decades as the 'age of legal aid, law reform, – and Lord Denning'. An even more effusive epithet came from a persistent litigant before Lord Denning, the kind of person called a public-spirited citizen when one agrees with him but a busy-body when one does not. Raymond Blackburn once described Lord Denning as the greatest living Englishman. This was hardly brave, in the presence of Lord Denning and in the course of asking him for costs and leave to appeal. Lord Denning enjoined him to 'Tell that to the House of Lords'.

Professor McAuslan has assessed Lord Denning thus:

> What Lord Mountbatten was to the Royals, Lord Denning is to the judiciary: unorthodox, larger than life, a great performer, eager to emphasize his own considerable contributions to public life.

Another academic wrote of

> the tragic drama of a great judge whose acute sense of rightness has become a conviction of righteousness, whose

consciousness of the need for justice has led him to become a self-appointed arbiter in the politics of society and whose desire to draw attention to defects in our law has more noticeably drawn attention to himself.

Lord Denning took to writing books about his career, the first being ironically entitled *The Discipline of the Law* and amounting to, as Lord Hailsham observed, a 'sort of *Festschrift* composed entirely by himself'. Eventually a book proved his undoing. One book made some injudicious comments about black jurors and his retirement was brought forward in the ensuing controversy. He ended his career on the Bench at the age of eighty-three. Lord Hailsham's farewell emphasized Lord Denning's courtesy and patience, good qualities for a judge, as well as, of course his innovative force:

> Master of the Rolls, we shall miss you. We shall miss your passion for justice, your independence and quality of thought, your liberal mind, your geniality, your unfailing courtesy to colleagues, to counsel, and to litigants in person.

Lord Denning, then, remains an enigma. But in our terms, he had a very clear appreciation of all three aspects of the law-making functions of a judge. He knew his way around the past law, he knew the importance of policy, and he had a crystal-clear vision that he would use the latter to trump the former when he saw the present law as unjust. On the policy point, he once said in *Enderby Town F.C. v. Football Association Ltd.* [1971] 1 Ch. 591:

> I know that over 300 years ago Hobart C.J. said that 'Public policy is an unruly horse'. It has often been repeated since. So unruly is the horse, it is said (per Burrough J in *Richardson v. Mellish* [1924]) that no judge should ever try to mount it lest it run away with him. I disagree. With a good man in the saddle, the unruly horse can be kept in control. It can jump over obstacles. It can leap the fences put up by fictions and come down on the side of justice.

Now, this image of Lord Denning as the Harvey Smith of the judiciary and the law as an unbridled horse has both good and bad aspects. The good is that everyone wants justice. The bad is that everyone disagrees on what justice determines so that we usually vote for politicians to chart the course which has most support within a democracy. On the other hand, a democracy ought also to protect the minorities from oppression by the majority so that judges have a valuable role in safeguarding our civil liberties. But in all this, one judge's view is not necessarily the right answer. We applaud Lord Denning when we agree with him, we decry him when we disagree. I think that we need to acknowledge Lord Denning's open endorsement of the creative role of the judges in the quest for justice but at the same time we must demand that judges consider more carefully the way in which they decide matters of public policy. It is not the relevance of social consequences which is in dispute but the accuracy of Lord Denning's assessment of the consequences.

Above all, I think that Lord Denning's idiosyncratic career on the Bench demonstrates a truth which most commentators miss. Dworkin and others seem to be seeking one right method for judges to employ. In the USA, there is a major disagreement between liberals on the Supreme Court, who seem preoccupied with our second, policy factor, and conservatives who claim that they are only interested in the original intent or historical intent of the founders of the American Constitution, the principles of our first factor. This is, of course, a dispute which I would locate within our third concern, the role of the judge. But my point here is that all the protagonists seem to assume that there is one right method, one right answer to the proper role for a judge. This is the central error of most jurisprudence on this topic. It seems to me that the proper answer to the role of the judge will vary through time, depending on what the other institutions of government are doing and indeed on what other judges are doing. Why have nine members of the Supreme Court if they are all meant to be copying one another? Surely, it is positively healthy for the judiciary to have different perceptions of their own role. That preserves the role of the judges in a state of tension and constant re-examination, which is vital when there are so few other constraints on judges. If we do not like the direction in which judges are heading, judges with a different view will be appointed. Equilibrium may be a false goal but we are deceiving ourselves if we think that identikit judges are the solution to the need for judicial law-making.

Thus, I think that it is possible, indeed desirable, to claim that one Lord Denning is a boon to a legal system, whereas a few hundred Lords Denning would have sacrificed too much certainty for too much Denning-justice. Lord Denning played a useful role in highlighting the question of the practical impact of old law on new cases and in his readiness to push the law in the direction of what he considered just consequences. In life after Lord Denning, it is difficult to pretend that judges do not have discretion (although not impossible, as Dworkin keeps on demonstrating).

Lord Devlin

———

Lord Devlin's judicial record is a matter of ancient history to today's law students who were born years after he had retired. He was one of the brightest judges of the century and certainly one of the youngest to reach successive stages of the judicial ladder. But he retired prematurely as a Law Lord at the age of fifty-seven in 1964, perhaps bored by the monotony of cases in the Lords, perhaps frustrated by not holding one of the powerful posts such as Master of the Rolls or Lord Chief Justice (his subsequent book on the trial of Dr Bodkin Adams, over which he presided as the judge, reveals his desire to have become Lord Chief Justice). He would not have been the only Law Lord to find the job tedious or frustrating. Lord Denning, for instance, preferred to go back to the Court of Appeal as Master of the Rolls where he could exercise more influence and have the more exciting job of handling a rapid turnover of cases.

Despite the lapse of time since he was on the Bench, Lord Devlin is none the less well known to law students and to a wider public. He sprang to prominence in jurisprudential terms with his Maccabaean Lecture in 1957 which criticized some of the reasoning (though not the recommendations) of the Wolfenden Report on homosexuality and prostitution. He stood up for society's right to protect its moral values through the law and attracted criticism from the leading British legal philosopher of the century, Professor H.L.A. Hart, who preferred to build on the classical liberal doctrine of John Stuart Mill that society should not coerce people through the law unless they were causing physical harm. Their exchange of views, culminating in books and perpetuated in student minds as the Hart-Devlin debate, makes Lord Devlin the only British judge of the century with a distinguished pedigree in legal philosophy.

Not content with this contribution, he has written extensively about judges themselves. His essays have been published in a volume entitled *The Judge*, in which he develops his thesis that judges should follow the consensus view in society. They need not be hidebound by precedent, so they can take account of policy as well as principle, of consequences as well as precedents. But Lord Devlin's conception of the judicial role is that the judges should only trump principle/precedent with policy/consequences when the policy or their assessment of the consequences reflects a consensus. They should not be dynamic law-makers, leading public opinion. That would be to usurp the role of elected politicians.

This seems a safe compromise. It is well put in his critique of Griffith. He has urged judges and others to read Griffith's attack but he does not himself find much to worry about in the Nightmare. He thinks that Griffith's complaint as to the background and age of the judges is one that could be levelled at more or less all the leaders of more or less all the professions. But his own vision of the judicial role does not allow judges the opportunity to impose their values, so he doubts whether the judges' class prejudices come into play. One reason for this which he points out is that judges are perhaps the most likely of people to be aware of their own and others' prejudices. Their training at the Bar, arguing on one side or the other, looking for biased jurors, and so on, all equips them for the necessary process of self-examination. If Griffith is right to imply that we all suffer from prejudices, he has not dealt with this response that judges have institutional conditioning which would make them more aware of any such tendencies. Putting them aside, they could then proceed to decide hard cases according to the consensus view in society rather than the view in their subconscious. One might add that academics like Griffith, Dworkin and myself might have fewer institutional reasons to recognize our own biases. Nevertheless, Lord Devlin thinks that it is always helpful to be reminded of the possibility of prejudice and thus thinks that judges would benefit from Griffith's scepticism.

But Devlin could himself be subjected to another Griffith point which the professor developed in a critique of Dworkin, namely that there is no consensus in society from which judges can derive the answers to hard cases. Lord Devlin, as in his debate with Hart, believes that a consensus exists. I am never quite sure how much agreement is needed for a 'consensus' but I tend on this point to share Griffith's scepticism. The danger is that what seems a consensus to the judge sitting in court might not seem a consensus to others outside. Nevertheless, the spirit of Lord Devlin's approach is at least to restrict the unbridled creativity of dynamic judges by reminding them that they should not be espousing their own concerns. They should rather be discerning the mood of the country. Is that not a good idea?

No, not really. If that were the right answer to our third quest, for the proper role for judges, then we would have to ask ourselves why we had judges at all. If we really want to know what the consensus is in society why not employ opinion pollsters? Why have lawyers in fancy dress ostensibly arguing about past cases if the septuagenarians on the Bench are really trying to second-guess the result of a national referendum?

It is on these jurisprudential contributions that we tend to judge Lord Devlin nowadays. He is not averse to giving his views on today's cases to the media. And some of his own decisions are models of the judicial art, although I do not propose to discuss them since they fail to meet my criteria for this book of being familiar and recent. But his legacy is the unusual one, for a judge, of his extra-judicial writing. How should we judge the judge's judging of judges?

Well, Lord Devlin has not finally answered our questions but he was at least asking questions along the right lines. He recognized that past law was not the only concern of the judge. He realized that judges could and should look at the impact of their decisions. In his debate with Professor Hart, he demonstrated a distinctive (if not always well received) approach to the question of evaluating the consequences of proposed laws. And he tried to solve the problem of differentiating their role from that of politicians with his distinction between dynamic and consensus law-making. Lord Devlin's contribution to our understanding of judicial decision-making deserves recognition in that he provided us with the building blocks for developing a theory even if we disagree with his own conclusions.

But even within his extra-judicial theorizing, it is not really his analysis of the judges as much as his analysis of the relationship between law and morality which will stand as his major jurisprudential achievement. Since this is very relevant to the second factor of evaluating the consequences of future law it is worth further consideration here. We turn to the Hart-Devlin debate.

The Wolfenden Report recommended the decriminalization of homosexual acts between consenting adults in private. Its justification was:

> the importance which society and the law ought to give to individual freedom of choice and action in matters of private morality. Unless a deliberate attempt is to be made by society, acting through the agency of the law, to equate the sphere of crime with that of sin, there must remain a realm of private morality which is, in brief and crude terms, not the law's business.

Now Lord Devlin's quarrel was not with the recommendations of the Wolfenden Report. Indeed, as a High Court judge he had given evidence suggesting that the law ought to be relaxed. But he had severe doubts about the wisdom of the quoted passage and similar statements as general guides to the relationship between law and morality.

Lord Devlin argued that society has the right to pass judgement on matters of morals. For it is precisely a 'shared morality' which makes a number of individuals into a 'society'. Thus, society has the right to use the law to enforce morality 'in the same way as it uses it to safeguard anything else that is essential to its existence'. Lord Devlin concluded that 'the suppression of vice is as much the law's business as the suppression of subversive activities'.

So why was he nevertheless in favour of, on this occasion, easing the law's restrictions? Lord Devlin explained that 'Nothing should be punished by the law that does not lie beyond the limits of tolerance' which are reached at a 'real feeling of revulsion', not merely a 'dislike' of a practice. Moreover, 'as far as possible privacy should be respected' and we should remember that 'The law is concerned with a minimum and not with a maximum standard of behaviour.'

Professor Hart criticized Lord Devlin in a radio talk which was published in *The Listener* and which was later developed into a book. Profesor Hart said that the question for debate was 'Is the fact that certain conduct is by common standards immoral sufficient to justify making that conduct punishable by law?' The professor assumed that Lord Devlin would answer yes whereas he answered no. Hart preferred John Stuart Mill's approach to these problems under which society should only intervene to 'prevent harm to others', although Hart adds a gloss to Mill in also justifying paternalistic intervention to prevent people from physically harming themselves.

The debate is still alive and well and I have discussed it elsewhere. But Lord Devlin's consistency (many would say his consistent mistake) emerges in what Hart calls Devlin's 'undiscussed assumption':

> This is that all morality – sexual morality together with the morality that forbids acts injurious to others such as killing, stealing and dishonesty – forms a single, seamless web, so that those who deviate from any part of it are likely or perhaps bound to deviate from the whole. It is of course clear (and one of the oldest insights of political theory) that society could not exist without a morality which mirrored and supplemented the law's proscription of conduct injurious to others. But there is again no evidence to support, and much to refute, the theory that those who deviate from conventional sexual morality are in other ways hostile to society.

In other words, there is no consensus or, at least, no consensus on sexual morality. That may well be the weakness of Lord Devlin's jurisprudence but his contribution has also had its strengths. In particular, he seems to recognize the truth that the law is not, cannot be, and should not be, morally neutral. Legislators and judges in their law-making capacity have to choose between competing moralities, not between morality and no-morality. Lord Devlin, as we know from his later work on judges, would not give the judiciary so much freedom in enforcing morality. They should defer to the alleged consensus. But he has at least recognized this moral element to the development of the law. I have tried to capture this aspect of adjudication by the second factor of evaluating consequences. Before the judge can determine the consensus, if that is the judge's aim, he must work out what is the likely consequence of his decision and then estimate society's moral evaluation of it. As I have indicated already, I am sceptical of Lord Devlin's idea that the judge is determining society's consensus. I doubt whether a consensus exists in the hard cases which have featured in this book. Even if it does, I doubt whether judges should be bound by it. But Lord Devlin has at least set us off on the right track. Judges are not merely applying the past law. They are bringing some judgement to bear on the pre-existing legal material. And Lord Devlin has performed a great service in emphasizing that these are moral choices and ones which require an appreciation of the different role of judges and legislators.

19

Lord Hailsham

———

'Some ass might make me Lord Chancellor, perhaps in 1970.' Thus spake Quintin Hogg in 1950 as he succeeded to the title of Viscount Hailsham of St Marylebone. Sure enough, in 1970, Edward Heath appointed him Lord Chancellor. Margaret Thatcher reappointed him in both 1979 and 1983. Asses or not, these very different Prime Ministers seem to have been satisfied with their Lord Chancellor. He was the only Cabinet minister to have remained in his post throughout the Heath Government and the first two Thatcher administrations. He was the longest serving Lord Chancellor this century. Was he a great judge?

'The Lord Chancellor is one of the strangest persons in the British Constitution' according to the Labour hereditary peer and radical barrister Lord Gifford QC. He is referring to the office rather than to any particular office-holder, I think, but he gives us an insight. The Lord Chancellor is not an ordinary judge.

The Lord Chancellorship's strangeness lies in the fact that the incumbent is a member of all three branches of government. He is in the executive as a Cabinet minister, he is the head of the judiciary and he is also the Speaker of the House of Lords in its legislative capacity.

Lord Hailsham has been a soldier and a lawyer, a philosopher and a judge. Even if he is not quite Rambo, Rumpole, Socrates or Solomon, the variety of his experience is perhaps captured by this range. Indeed, he has even wider talents, as demonstrated by his formidable record as an administrator. Even so, none of this quite captures the man. He is, above all, a politician. And in all these roles he is an advocate, a Cicero.

His legal expertise dates from the age of seven. His father, himself twice a Lord Chancellor, lulled him to sleep with stories of his day in court (lawyers often lull people to sleep with such stories but in this case it was the sleep of the just and committed, not the sleep of the bored and disaffected). Young Quintin, never bashful about his own intellectual prowess, took it all in: 'I knew the whole complicated law of defamation long before I had learned the easiest lessons of mathematics.' He returned to the subject in his early twenties and taught himself law in a year's intense study for the All Souls examinations.

As a philosopher, he had a good grounding through his study of 'Greats' at university and his time at All Souls. His philosophical monuments are two books, *The Case for Conservatism*, first published in 1947, which is an impressive theoretical and practical statement of Tory convictions, and his semi-autobiographical work, *The Door Wherein I Went* (1975), which contains some valuable philosophical and theological thoughts. In the latter book, he also explains the basis of his intellectual prowess:

> I acquired, and have retained, an almost unlimited capacity to absorb information, great power of concentration, and meticulous habits of scholarship, marred only by the occasional carelessness caused by the speed at which I work. I was academically exceptionally gifted, and being intensely ambitious and competitive by nature, made full use of this gift.

Even though he would be the first (or, as he might put it, the Double First) to agree, one cannot deny that he is one of the most intelligent people in the country. In this respect, he followed a fine tradition of brilliant intellectuals as Lord Chancellors, perhaps the brightest and most famous of his predecessors being Thomas More and Francis Bacon.

As a soldier, Quintin Hogg fought in the Second World War. Although he was an MP, he immediately joined the army in September 1939, and later led an infantry platoon in battle before being wounded in action. The actor David Niven, in his autobiography *The Moon's a Balloon*, records another aspect to Lord Hailsham's war effort: 'When at the War Office, I shared a desk with a portly amiable captain who coped tirelessly and uncomplainingly with the mountainous paper work – Quintin Hogg.'

As a politician, Lord Hailsham had an eventful career. In 1938 he entered Parliament as an MP. After his active service, he joined the wartime government as an Under-Secretary for Air. His next ministerial appointment was to become the First Lord of the Admiralty in Eden's Government. Thereafter he became Minister of Education in Macmillan's first administration and went on to establish a reputation as Macmillan's troubleshooter. First, he became party chairman and masterminded Macmillan's third win in 1959. His exploits at the 1957 Brighton Conference have passed into folklore. If he was not ringing bells, he was swimming in the sea or otherwise capturing the media's attention.

Lord Hailsham's work in his next cabinet post, as Minister for Science and Technology, was later recognized when he was elected a Fellow of the Royal Society. Then he was off again as Macmillan's envoy, embarking on a series of special assignments for the Government, becoming Minister for Sport, then Minister for the North-East, then chief negotiator of the Nuclear Test Ban Treaty. Since he does not enjoy watching sport and abominates sporting chauvinism, since he was not particularly well acquainted personally with the North-East or with unemployment, and since he was not renowned as a diplomat, he seems a surprising choice for these three roles. But in all these jobs, just as with the party chairmanship, what was needed was an advocate. And Lord Hailsham has always been a good advocate.

Lord Hailsham was Macmillan's choice to succeed him as Tory leader and therefore Prime Minister. Yet he failed to secure the leadership. Why? Perhaps he had been too good an advocate for Macmillan at the expense of his own appearance of *gravitas*. Perhaps he was just too much of a risk, too clever by half.

Whatever the reason, he still went ahead with the process of disclaiming his peerage and returned to the Bar as plain Quintin Hogg after Alec Douglas-Home's defeat in the 1964 election. He had had an illustrious political career, holding posts such as Lord Privy Seal, Lord President of the Council, and Leader of both the Commons and the Lords, in addition to the departmental responsibilities already mentioned. It was now time to concentrate on his legal practice and perhaps fulfil his ambition to become a judge.

But he could not leave politics alone. Although his legal practice flourished, he still managed to combine it with being a vigorous Shadow Home Secretary in Edward Heath's opposition team. He also found time to ridicule, and annoy, the judges in the magazine *Punch*.

When he did achieve his ambition to become a judge, it was through Heath appointing him as Lord Chancellor. When the Government fell in 1974, Lord Hailsham was still entitled to sit as a Law Lord and occasionally did so. But he busied himself in writing. He became a passionate advocate of constitutional reform, seeking better ways for the constitution to control what he dubbed the 'elective dictatorship'. But, to his evident surprise, his political career was far from over. In 1979, Mrs Thatcher invited him to resume responsibility as Lord Chancellor. He rejoined the elective dictatorship himself.

What was he like as a judge? As Lord Chancellor, of course, he moved straight from arguing cases as a barrister to having the right to sit as a member of the Judicial Committee of the House of Lords. His reputation as a judge is somewhat mixed. The burdens of office did not allow him to sit as a judge as often as he would have liked. He cut down his tedious responsibilities as Speaker of the House of Lords by delegating the job as much as possible. He also pruned the Lord Chancellor's involvement in Cabinet committees. So he spent most of his time running the Lord Chancellor's Department which has responsibility for, among other things, the appointment of judges, the provision of courts, procedure in courts, the legal aid scheme and reform of the law in general. Formally, it is the Prime Minister who decides on promotions to the Court of Appeal or to join the Law Lords, whereas the Lord Chancellor selects the lower ranks of the judiciary himself. But, in practice, the Prime Minister accepts his recommendations.

Was he good at all this? Lord Hailsham came under fire from the legal professions on a variety of issues, in particular over their remuneration for legal aid work. Non-lawyers, on the other hand, tended to think that he was too deferential to his own profession. If criticism from all quarters is a sign of balance, perhaps he did very well indeed.

What Lord Hailsham really objected to was criticism of the judges from the media and from the House of Commons. He thinks that the judges should by and large maintain a dignified silence and let their judgments and bearing, in open court after all, speak for themselves. I think this is misguided in the modern world. The media are more interested in judges than ever before. There is more danger in uninformed ignorance than in dialogue between judges and judged. The Lord Chancellor should have used his real talents as an advocate to explain the judicial process to the ever-more-interested public. In *The Door Wherein I Went*, for example, he makes the point well:

> Impartiality does not consist in having no controversial opinions or even prejudices. The Bench is not made up of political, religious or social neuters. Impartiality consists in the capacity to be aware of one's subjective opinions and to place them on one side when one enters the professional field, and the ability to listen patiently to and to weigh evidence and argument and to withhold concluded judgment until the case is over.

But Lord Hailsham chose to continue the 'Kilmuir Rules' under which a blanket of silence was accepted by the judges unless the Lord Chancellor gives his permission for them to talk to the media. This did not apply to the Law Lords at the top of the judicial hierarchy. Much lower down the tree, Judge Pickles thought that it should not apply to him whereas Lord Hailsham (and the rest of the Bench) thought it most definitely should.

The Lord Chancellor's power over judges, through the right to appoint and promote, is becoming a controversial political issue. The Opposition parties have been calling for a Minister of Justice and a Select Committee on Legal Affairs to take over the Lord Chancellor's mantle. Lord Hailsham has said that this would be 'utterly deplorable' and a 'threat to the independence of the judges which is the bulwark of our liberties'. Yet Lord Hailsham has himself been supportive of other constitutional reform in the past. It might seem that his enthusiasm for reform of the electoral system, of the House of Lords in its legislative capacity and for a Bill of Rights has oscillated. When in Opposition he wrote in favour of reform, when in power he was strangely silent. Lord Hailsham would say, however, that his opinions did not change in such a pragmatic way, but his willingness to *express* his own convictions did oscillate; depending on whether he was in or out of government, they had to be tempered by certain restraints on a Cabinet minister.

But all this is Hailsham the politician. Let us return to the issue of his performance as a judge. His cases provide a very limited sample, numbering only a couple of dozen compared to Lord Denning's couple of thousand. Like Lord Denning within the Court of Appeal, however, Lord Hailsham could at least choose which House of Lords cases to sit on, although it would have been imprudent for the Lord Chancellor to sit on cases which were controversial in a party political sense. He chose in particular to sit on criminal appeals, apparently relishing the difficult questions of the philosophy of mind which these cases involve. 'What is intention?', for example, is a question which probably intrigued Hailsham the philosopher and one which recurs in criminal appeals.

One should perhaps add a caveat here. Many lawyers feel that the House of Lords is at its worst in these criminal cases. There may be a good argument for leaving the Court of Appeal as the last resort in these matters. Appeals have hitherto been one-sided, viz. a right in the defence but not the prosecution, the force of which is to give the accused the benefit of any doubt but which is perhaps an odd method for clarifying the law. More importantly, the question will be: did the judge err in his summing up to a jury? Now, the cleverest lawyers in the kingdom, including the Law Lords, are not necessarily the best people to direct a jury. Law Lords have seldom come from a criminal practice and have seldom heard many criminal cases and have seldom even seen a jury within a decade. The Lord Chief Justice, on the other hand, who runs the criminal side of the courts culminating in the Criminal Division of the Court of Appeal, actually goes out and tries cases and talks extensively to the judges who do so. Thus the Court of Appeal may have a closer feel for what is appropriate in a direction to lay jurors. A frightfully clever piece of metaphysics in the House of Lords may not always produce the desired result when transmitted to the jury, once described as twelve people of average ignorance.

That said, Lord Hailsham did make a series of decisions which baffled lower judges and which came back to the Lords for further elucidation. His judgment in a case on attempting the impossible in the law of theft was described by the leading criminal law professor as 'technically the worst decision of the House of Lords this century'. His judgments in murder cases similarly exasperated criminal lawyers. In one such case, *Moloney*, he felt compelled to defend his earlier judgment in *Hyam* in a passage which perhaps conveys the complexities of the area, or at least of Lord Hailsham's judgments:

> I certainly did not intend by my observations to fall either into the trap of opening up a charge of murder in 'murder manslaughter' cases which are the result of criminal negligence or recklessness and not intention, or to excuse the hypothetical terrorist in my noble and learned friend's bomb disposal case whose intention may well prove to have been obvious . . . I do not think I fell into either error. But, if I did, I would have clearly been wrong.

The thrust of Lord Bridge's speech in *Moloney*, with whom the other Law Lords agreed, was that Lord Hailsham had been clever in *Hyam* at the expense of being simple. As Lord Bridge said, Lord Hailsham's speech was 'supported by the most convincing jurisprudential and philosophical arguments to be found in any of the speeches in *Hyam*. But I have to add at once that there are two reasons why I cannot regard it as providing practical guidance to judges who have to direct juries . . .' Of course, Lord Hailsham never had directed a jury in his life, having gone straight in as a judge to the House of Lords. Indeed, in one of those attempting-the-impossible cases (can you be guilty of receiving stolen goods or of possessing heroin if you mistakenly thought that was what you were doing but where in fact the goods were not stolen or the 'heroin' was snuff?), *Haughton v. Smith*, he himself warned of the dangers of over-analysis before proceeding to over-analyse. Then in *R. v. Shivpuri* he seemed to blame Parliament for failing to bury his speech in *Haughton*.

But perhaps it would be fairer to take a 1987 decision of the Law Lords as an example of Lord Hailsham's judicial technique, namely *R. v. Howe*, a case on whether duress should be a defence to the crime of murder. Lord Hailsham clearly understood more than most the interaction of past legal principle, future consequences and judicial role in reaching the conclusion that duress should not be a defence to murder.

Howe strangled a youth but claimed that he was acting under duress in that he was obeying the instructions of a man he feared, a man who would have strangled Howe himself if he had disobeyed. A previous House of Lords decision, *Lynch v. DPP of Northern Ireland* (1975) had, by a 3-2 majority, allowed duress as a defence for those people who aided and abetted a murder (principals in the second degree). But it had been strongly criticized and this was, in any event, murder by a principal in the first degree (the actual killer). As Lord Hailsham observed, *Howe* 'affords an ideal and never to be repeated opportunity to consider, as we were expressly invited to do so by the Crown, the whole question afresh, if necessary by applying the 1966 Practice Statement to the decision in *Lynch*'s case'.

Lord Hailsham took the opportunity to reconsider the matter and was prepared to apply the Practice Statement. He surveyed the past law, looking not only at *Lynch* but also at earlier cases and academic opinion. He thus showed that it was the majority view in *Lynch* which was out of step with the principle of the pre-existing common law: 'to say the least, prior to Lynch's case there was a heavy preponderance of authority against the availability of duress in cases of murder'.

But that was not all that mattered. Lord Hailsham continued by looking at the consequences of the alternative possible conclusions and rejected the argument that, in relation to the defence of duress to the crime of murder:

> it is either good morals, good policy or good law to suggest, as did the majority in *Lynch* . . . that the ordinary man of reasonable fortitude is not to be supposed to be capable of heroism if he is asked to take an innocent life rather than sacrifice his own.

One consequence of the decision would be the mandatory life sentence. Lord Hailsham saw this consequence but did not find it unpalatable, preferring to rely on the Executive to release prisoners early if 'the law seems to bear harshly in its operation . . . on any particular offender'.

Lord Hailsham's mind was firmly set on some other

consequences: 'We live in the age of the Holocaust of the Jews, of international terrorism on the scale of massacre, of the explosion of aircraft in mid-air.' Lord Hailsham was not prepared to allow a defence of duress to become a terrorists' charter. In all these circumstances, Lord Hailsham was able to undermine the legal pedigree of *Lynch* and simultaneously to point out its undesirable consequences. He therefore saw his role as being to reject the claim of duress.

Lord Hailsham was a shrewd enough lawyer to know that a variety of factors influence a decision such as this to overrule a precedent. He could have been a good judge but he will be remembered primarily for the non-judicial (and some would say injudicious) events of his political career. He was a politician first and a judge second. He was succeeded, briefly, by Lord Havers who did not have the time to sit as a judge before ill-health quickly forced him to resign. Then came Lord Mackay as the third Lord Chancellor of the year, a man who was more a judge first and a politician second.

20

Lord Mackay

———

In 1987, Lord Chancellors came and went almost at the rate of Supreme Court nominees. But while the American public was presented with detailed analyses of Judges Bork, Ginsburg and Kennedy, little attention has been paid in the United Kingdom to the judicial records of Lords Hailsham, Havers and Mackay.

There are at least three explanations. Since we have no chance to influence their confirmation or rejection, some would say there is no point in examining the judicial performance of Lord Chancellors. Furthermore, since Lords Hailsham and Havers had no prior experience as senior judges, there was not much evidence to analyse when they were appointed. And since recent Lord Chancellors have not spent much time sitting in their judicial capacity, some would argue that it does not matter much whether or not they are good judges.

But we do have lots of evidence of Lord Mackay's judicial technique and the evidence is so encouraging that we must hope that he will continue to sit. Moreover, his reputation as a judge, allied to his powers as Lord Chancellor (viz. of appointment and promotion – to hire and 'higher' judges, although not to fire the senior ones) might encourage others to follow his style of judging.

Lord Mackay's appointment has rightly been welcomed on various grounds. Everybody now knows that Scottish judges are allegedly more interested in principle than precedent, or so Lord McCluskey has been saying in homage to his new boss ('Scots law . . . is a system sustained by principle, not one shackled by precedent'). Everybody has also been welcoming his spirit of *glasnost* in abandoning the Kilmuir Rules. (Although one would have thought that the very title *Kilmuir* Rules, referring to the former Lord Chancellor who on departing the Woolsack in a Macmillan-propelled hurry was rewarded with the title of Earl

Kilmuir and Baron Fyfe of Dornoch, would stop people from claiming mistakenly that Lord Mackay is the first Scottish Lord Chancellor.)

So what are the hallmarks of Lord Mackay's judicial style? First, this Conservative Lord Chancellor has disproved Griffith's thesis by leading the Law Lords to impeccably progressive decisions in two important cases within his first few months in office. In *Polkey* he made it much more difficult for employers to justify a procedurally unfair dismissal by claiming that the employee deserved to be dismissed anyway. Then in *Hayward v. Cammell Laird*, he opened up the floodgates for claims of unequal pay through sex discrimination. The Law Lords allowed an appeal from the Court of Appeal so that a woman who worked in Cammell Laird's canteen could claim the same basic rate of pay as men in their shipyard who undertook work of equal value, even though she was preferentially treated with regard to other terms and conditions of employment.

Second, he is prepared to say what he thinks. If he is not going to give a full opinion, he often at least adds a pertinent paragraph instead of relying on the formula that there is nothing one can usefully add. In particular, judges ought to regard themselves as under a duty to explain exactly why they differ from one another when there is a dissent. Their Lordships' failure to do this in *Anderton v.Ryan*, on attempting the impossible, allowed them to escape the conclusion that Lord Edmund-Davies was right to dissent. That matter had to be resolved by the House of Lords having another bite at the cherry in *R. v. Shivpuri*, with Lord Mackay spelling out on what points he was agreeing with Lord Hailsham and on what points he was agreeing with Lord Bridge in preference to the former Lord Chancellor.

Third, Lord Mackay is willing to take account of academic views, an openness which is bound to appeal to academics but which is, more importantly, constructive in the joint task of developing the law. Perhaps the best of academic views are often filtered through the Law Commission, hence his reference to the Commission in *R. v. Howe* (the duress case). Lord Mackay's opinion here is interesting, however, not only for its detailed treatment of the academic and Law Commission material. Perhaps his Scottish roots emerge most clearly here in his affection for the Scottish criminal law writer, Hume, who it transpires said all that needed to be said a long time ago.

The fourth feature of Lord Mackay's judgments concerns Lord McCluskey's point that Scottish judges rely on principle. We all like to believe in principle, none more so than Ronald Dworkin, but some of us find that there are too many principles competing for our belief, so that the judge still has to play a creative role which is motivated in large part by the justice of the case or the 'policy' factors it involves. In the Northern Irish case of *O'Sullivan v. Herdmans Ltd* [1987], for instance, Lord Mackay dismissed an appeal against an order for discovery against a third party for medical records to help resolve a personal injuries dispute. He was well aware of the policies or consequences at stake and took a no-nonsense approach to arguments that he should adopt a restrictive interpretation of the court's powers:

> The interests of justice are, in my opinion, served by the promotion of early settlements rather than the prolongation of litigation and by the possibility of early, complete preparation for both parties to a trial rather than by obliging one party to delay its full preparation until after the trial has actually started.

Anybody can pluck principles out of thin air yet what we really want are judges who are meticulous in explaining whence the principle came in the case-law and whither it is going in the real world. In this regard, I am delighted to report that Lord Mackay's judgments are exhaustive analyses of previous case-law to determine the 'principle' which underlies the precedents. In the Scottish case of *Smith v. Littlewoods* [1987] (negligence involving a fire on a property (caused by arson) damaging another property), for example, Lord Mackay's quest for principle takes him most usefully through innumerable cases. We can all accept the thrust of Lord McCluskey's praise for principle and suspicion of the technicalities of precedent if the judges take pains to distil the principles accurately from the raw material of previous decisions and if they have a shrewd grasp of how to choose between competing principles by reference to the impact they will have on today's society. Lord Mackay passes these tests with flying colours.

A fifth attractive feature of Lord Mackay's judgments is that he is prepared to look at comparative law for help, not just the comparison between Scotland and England but even further afield. In *Hotson v. East Berkshire* [1987], on causation in negligence cases of personal injuries, Lord Mackay with evident relish sets out on an analysis of a decision by the Supreme Court of the state of Washington. His horizons stretch beyond the borders between the English and Scottish legal systems.

Lord Mackay's Maccabaean Lecture in 1987, shortly after his appointment to the Woolsack, explored whether we have anything to learn from the US legal system in a more dramatic sense, as he considered the American doctrine of prospective overruling. His interest in this topic, and the title of his lecture, 'Can judges change the law?' suggest my sixth point, that Lord Mackay has the necessary appreciation of the importance of judges assessing their own role in the constitution. Even if there are suggestions that he has sympathy with the beguiling McCluskey/Dworkinian route of emphasizing principle (which I believe is attractive, nay flattering, to the judges but ultimately too narrow in apparently excluding the relevance of policy arguments when judges are often second-guessing Parliament), even that position presupposes a certain view of the role of judges in a democracy. Our judges must articulate their own conceptions of their role. Indeed, Lord Mackay has already shown an appreciation of the strengths and limitations of the judicial role in law-making. In the duress case, *R. v. Howe*, he pays homage to Lord Reid, a good mentor for a Scottish judge and former Lord Advocate, quoting Lord Reid's words of wisdom in *Myers v. DPP* [1965] (written before the 1966 Practice Statement which freed their Lordships from always following their previous decisions):

> I have never taken a narrow view of the functions of this House as an appellate tribunal. The common law must be developed to meet changing economic conditions and habits of thought, and I would not be deterred by expressions of opinion in this House in old cases. But there are limits to what we can or should do. If we are to extend the law it must be by the development and application of fundamental principles . . . If we are to give a wide interpretation to our

judicial functions questions of policy cannot be wholly excluded, and it seems to me against public policy to produce uncertainty.

Lord Mackay repeated this quotation while showing again an appreciation of the arguments about judicial decision-making in his Maccabaean Lecture. He mentioned some well-known juris-prudential names, such as Austin, Bentham, Hart, Dworkin and Sartorius (well, he included some just-about-known names). Of judges, Lords Diplock and Devlin received honourable mentions but, not surprisingly, it was Lord Reid who figured most prominently as the fount of judicial wisdom.

I would expect Lord Mackay to encourage, by his judicial and judicious example, and his appointments and promotions, his colleagues on the Bench to steer a creative course between the Scylla of a rigid adherence to the past and the Charybdis of an uncertain future for our legal system. And I suspect that he will urge his Cabinet and legislative colleagues to help the judges by taking on those areas of law reform which are too dramatic for judges to explore in a single case. His Maccabaean Lecture made it clear that he has respect for the role of the Law Commissions and feels that their rise has reduced the scope for judicial creativity. The Lord Chancellor agreed with Lord Scarman 'that Parliament should give favourable consideration to Bills based on recommen-dations of the Law Commission' and thought that 'it was certainly arguable that since the two Law Commissions were established, for the purpose of promoting reform of the law, the opportunities for judge-made law have become fewer'. One might add a proviso there, namely *if* Parliament can be persuaded to pay attention to Law Commission recommendations and if the Law Commissions can cover sufficient areas of the law which need such reform.

But at least this was part of a running theme in Lord Mackay's lecture of the constitutional distinctions between judicial and parliamentary law-making, and a distinct preference for the latter. Lord Mackay's question was 'Can judges change the law?' His answer was 'yes'. But the sub-theme of the latter part of the lecture was whether they could use the device of prospective overruling in changing the law. The answer here was 'no', which at least absolves me from explaining the doctrine to those who do not understand it. As Lord Goff, who chaired the lecture, wisely observed in summing-up, 'All judges now know where they stand: no prospective overruling.'

Lord Mackay's worries about prospective overruling followed the pattern of Lord Devlin's famous asseertion that it crossed the Rubicon between judicial and legislative development of the law. It is acceptable to paddle across the river under disguise ('perhaps that is the reason for our robes' joked the Lord Chancellor) but not to bridge the river with bands playing.

How can judges change the law, then? Lord Mackay concluded with his answer: 'If judges are to change the law, and I see no reason to conceal the fact that they do, it must be by the development and application of fundamental principles to disputes between parties concerned about specific events which have occurred in the past.'

The lecture began and ended, therefore, with an important and explicit rejection of the fairy tale. The Nightmare was not dignified by even meriting consideration. He flirted with the Noble Dream but at the level of rhetoric rather than practice. In his actual judgments, Lord Mackay is firmly rooted in a balanced appreciation of the various issues involved in judicial decision-making.

21

Lord Scarman

———

Was Lord Scarman a great judge? He is certainly more than just another judge. His contributions to British law and government have been multifarious and important. He has undertaken four major inquiries for various governments, into the troubles of Northern Ireland, Red Lion Square, Grunwick and, most famously, Brixton. He was the first and most influential Chairman of the Law Commission which recommends law reform. He has been, and indeed still is, an active member of the House of Lords in its legislative capacity, arguing vigorously, for example, in favour of amendments to the Police and Criminal Evidence Bill in 1984. He is the leading advocate of constitutional reform, urging us to incorporate the European Convention on Human Rights into our domestic law as a Bill of Rights. As a judge in the High Court, he helped develop our family law (capping this at the Law Commission by recommending what became the revolutionary Divorce Reform Act of 1969). He was then promoted to the Court of Appeal where he spent the mid-1970s, when that court was at its most interesting period under the control of Lord Denning. In 1977 he was elevated to the House of Lords and participated in many of the Law Lords' most controversial cases, such as the *Gay News* blasphemy decision, the Fares Fair litigation over Ken Livingstone's GLC, the GCHQ dispute between the Prime Minister and the unions, and the Gillick case about teenage contraception, before retiring in 1986 as he approached the age of seventy-five.

How good was he as a judge and why was he so great and good as to be frequently chosen from the serried ranks of public worthies to report into problem after problem?

The answer to both questions is perhaps revealed by his own first thoughts when asked about the judicial role. 'The judge's job', he insisted, 'is to listen. Witnesses should be given every opportunity to settle down and say what they have to say in the way they want to say it.' Some other judges would prefer, one suspects, to think of the judge's task as to be frighteningly clever. But Lord Scarman, who is of course frighteningly clever himself, has the rare gift of putting witnesses at their ease, making them feel that their contributions are important, and thus winning their confidence in the impartiality of his judgment. This skill has served him particularly well outside the courtroom, as when he listened to the people of Brixton in 1981.

Some have suspected that he is too committed to liberal principles to be the perfectly impartial judge. The record tends to show, however, that he is too committed to judicial principles to be the perfect liberal. It is not always obvious which way a liberal would want to decide cases. If a 'liberal' would have found for Ken Livingstone in the Fares Fair case or against the Prime Minister in the GCHQ case, then Lord Scarman cannot be reckoned a 'liberal'. In both cases he was party to unanimous decisions although one suspects that he must have at least toyed with the idea of dissenting in the GCHQ controversy. But how does one tell whether these or other decisions are illiberal?

When *Gay News*, as we have seen, was prosecuted for blasphemous libel in publishing a poem and illustration depicting Christ as a homosexual, Lord Scarman was the junior Law Lord on the case. Two of his seniors thought that the prosecution should have to show that *Gay News* actually intended to outrage Christians. The other two Law Lords thought that it was enough that the material was blasphemous, whether or not the paper intended to blaspheme. The outcome of the case thus depended on Lord Scarman's opinion. Many would feel that a 'liberal' would take a lenient view and brush aside this scurrilous poem without condemning it as a criminal offence. But remember how Lord Scarman decided against *Gay News*, beginning, 'My Lords, I do not subscribe to the view that the common law offence of blasphemous libel serves no useful purpose in the modern law. On the contrary, I think there is a case for legislation extending it to protect the religious beliefs and feelings of non-Christians.' That first sentence seems to herald an 'illiberal' opinion but the second seeks to challenge one's vision of where liberals should stand on the issue.

Three other characteristics of Lord Scarman's judicial career provide insights into the qualities of a great judge. First, his skill in finding and succinctly stating the facts is a necessary attribute of the good lawyer. Whether the lawyer is a solicitor listening to a client telling the story of a marital breakdown or Lord Scarman listening to contradictory accounts of the Brixton riots, it is essential to separate the relevant from the irrelevant and the truth from the fiction. Under Lord Scarman's chairmanship, a tribunal of three produced in 1972 a masterly exposition of myth and reality in relation to the troubles of Northern Ireland (this is, sadly, a widely unread document but it is worth tracking down – Cmnd (N.I.)566). Lord Scarman on his own produced a definitive summary of events leading up to and during the 1981 Brixton riots.

Second, once the facts have been found and if the law to be applied to them is not cut and dried, then the judge must have some vision of his role in developing the law. Legal philosophers have spent much time in analysing how judicial discretion should be exercised. Lord Denning had no truck with this scholarship, declaring that 'the jargon of the philosophers of the law has always been beyond me'. But Lord Scarman has thought deeply and read widely in jurisprudence, greeting me, when I interviewed him in the summer of 1986, with the question had I 'read Ronnie Dworkin's latest book, *Law's Empire*?' We both had read it, Lord Scarman with greater interest perhaps because he features in the book as the British judge who comes nearest to Dworkin's ideal. Lord Scarman has been convinced by Dworkin. So much so that Lord Scarman has apparently abandoned his interest in policy, which we saw in the *Gay News* case. He has instead, as we saw in Gillick articulated a Dworkinian approach to adjudication in recent cases. The idea is that the judge's role is to undertake a quest for the principles which underlie the law. The judge should not decide according to his own vision of the most desirable policy for the law to adopt. That would be usurping the role of the legislature which is best placed to balance competing visions of what public policy demands. The judicial forum is and should be one of principle. I do not myself believe that one can draw such a clear distinction between principle and policy, nor that judges need to do so. Nevertheless, I applaud Lord Scarman's openness to jurisprudential ideas and his willingness to define the judicial function.

Third, having established the facts and the law, the judge has to communicate all this to the litigants, their lawyers, the wider legal community, and the general public. These diverse audiences test the judges' command of language. Lord Scarman not only conveys his views in a manner which all can understand but he does so with great style.

Many of the above points can be illustrated by two cases which were in every way the culmination of his judicial career: *Sidaway* and *Gillick*. In the former, Lord Scarman set English law on course towards a doctrine of informed consent as a prerequisite of medical treatment. In the latter, he laid down the principles which will guide our law towards a proper respect for children's rights. His *Gillick* judgment, in particular, deserves to be read as a masterpiece of English legal prose, even by those who disagree with his conclusions:

> The case is the beginning, not the conclusion of a legal development in a field glimpsed by one or two judges in recent times . . . but not yet fully explored . . . Women have obtained by the availability of the pill a choice of life-style with a degree of independence and of opportunity undreamed of until this generation and greater, I would add, than any law of equal opportunity could by itself effect. The law ignores these tasks at its peril. The House's task, therefore, as the supreme court in a legal system largely based on rules of law evolved over the years by the judicial process, is to search the overfull and cluttered shelves of the law reports for a principle, or set of principles recognized by the judges over the years but stripped of the detail which, however appropriate in their day, would, if applied today, lay the judges open to a justified criticism for failing to keep the law abreast of the society in which they live and work . . . If the law should impose upon the process of 'growing up' fixed limits where nature knows only a continuous process, the price would be artificiality and a lack of

realism in an area where the law must be sensitive to human development and social change.

All these skills – enthusiasm, sensitivity, willingness to listen, fact-finding, sense of purpose and ability to communicate – have applications beyond the courtroom. Not surprisingly, therefore, Lord Scarman has been repeatedly asked to put them to use in other arenas.

The central dilemma in evaluating Lord Scarman's extra-judicial career is whether it is right in a democracy for an unelected individual to wield so much power. He is, for instance, a member of the House of Lords in its legislative capacity by virtue of being a member of its judicial capacity. Apart from the Law Lords, the other legislators in our Upper House are there because of birth (the hereditary peers) or Prime Ministerial preferment as a life peer or as a senior Anglican bishop. This seems a somewhat motley crew for a legislative chamber. Does Lord Scarman support this unelected House? 'Yes. In theory, the House of Lords is a standing abuse but in fact it is a great bastion of our liberties.' The House of Lords works. Lord Scarman feels that it is very valuable to have institutions in the Constitution which are not dependent on a General Election for survival.

One of the noblest attempts of the Noble House to check the perhaps reckless rush of the Commons came with the Lords' review of the legislation to abolish the GLC and the metropolitan authorities. That, ultimately unsuccessful, struggle demonstrated the utility of a revising chamber which is beholden to nobody. It also demonstrated, to Lord Scarman at least, the fragility of our constitutional arrangements. He would welcome a constitutional settlement along American or Continental lines, which establishes a role for local government, be it a major or a minor one, and then protects it from the whim of central government. The Lords have indeed provided more of a challenge to the present Conservative Government than has the Commons. Lord Scarman does not make a practice of dividing the House of Lords against the Government but when he does he ultimately wins. He spoke in favour of amendments to the Police and Criminal Evidence Bill in 1984, for example, and the Government eventually accepted his proposal for a disciplinary offence for the police of racially prejudiced conduct. This was a matter close to his heart, of course, after the Brixton Report.

As for the fate of the Brixton Report itself, Lord Scarman is sanguine. He was pleased with the reception of his analysis. He thinks that the report has helped us all to understand better the problems but he does not pretend that there are easy solutions. As the great listener-judge, however, he does regret the move by some politicians and community leaders to boycott the consultative committees which have been established by statute upon his recommendation. It is a tragedy for Lord Scarman when channels of communication are obstructed.

His Red Lion Square Report was also well received. Its emphasis on balance between freedom and expression for protestors and peace and order for others has become the conventional wisdom on the law of public order and helped achieve the better parts of the Public Order Act (1986).

Although the House of Lords as a legislative chamber is performing valiantly, Lord Scarman is not content to let our Constitution muddle along in its traditional way. He is especially concerned to see us adopt a Bill of Rights (in effect, incorporating the European Convention on Human Rights into British law). This would, of course, give his successors in the judiciary even greater influence than they now possess. They would be able to strike down statutes which conflicted with the Bill of Rights and it would be the judges' interpretation of the Bill of Rights which counted. Why should unelected judges have such power? Lord Scarman's vision of democracy is one in which minorities' rights are protected against oppression from the majority. If we feel that there is a danger of such oppression in the UK, if we are confident that we know what rights to protect, if court procedure were adapted to suit this exercise, and if we trust judges other than Lord Scarman to interpret such a document sympathetically, there might be something in this. Otherwise, we might prefer to put our faith in political pressure and recognize that rights have to be claimed in the political arena.

Whether or not one agrees with his solution, Lord Scarman has identified the problem with his customary insight and eloquence:

When times are normal and fear is not stalking the land, English law sturdily protects the freedom of the individual and respects human personality. But when times are abnormally alive with fear and prejudice, the common law is at a disadvantage: it cannot resist the will, however frightened and prejudiced it may be, of Parliament.

Moreover, in many ways Lord Scarman is encouraging lawyers to prepare for a more central role in society. He does not see law and politics as separate fiefdoms. His own example shows that the two are inextricably linked. He has urged legal academics and indeed teachers throughout higher education to offer the young a broad-based experience. (His knowledge of that world is not confined to his own time as a classics scholar in Oxford; he has had broader experience himself in such roles as Chancellor of Warwick University, Chairman of the Court of London University and Chairman of the Council of Legal Education.) He wants legal practitioners, academics and students to open their eyes and look at what other disciplines have to offer and at what is best in the American and European legal traditions.

In short, he is intent on breaking down barriers in society, whether between lawyers and politicians, judges and the public, Protestants and Catholics, police and citizens, black and white. He comes from the background one associates with traditional judges – public school, Oxford, a First in Greats, a long and happy marriage, an informed enthusiasm for the arts, especially opera, and so on. But he has done his best to understand those from different backgrounds and to help them to understand one another. He rejects the attitude of judges who seek to insulate themselves from society through preserving the mystique of the law. That has led him into the public eye to such an extent that he would certainly fail the 'Mackinnon test'. In 1940, Lord Justice Mackinnon wrote that 'he is the best judge whose name is known to fewest readers of the *Daily Mail*'. Lord Scarman's twenty-five years as a judge constitute a powerful dissent from that narrow view.

So how does Lord Scarman rate in terms of our criteria? He endeavoured to explore the past law in a Dworkinian quest for principle. He gave the impression that he was ignoring policy, although (like Dworkin) he usually found a principle to suit what would probably have been his intuitive assessment of the best policy direction for the law to take. He was, more than most judges, aware of the issue of his own role. His judgments in *Duport Steels v. Sirs* and in *Gillick* are eloquent testimony to his appreciation of the problem. Far more than other judges of his generation, he realized that he had to find a niche for his own role in our democracy which dovetailed with the functions of elected politicians. In my opinion, however, he adopted too readily Dworkin's vision of the judicial role. It is easy to see how that might happen. Lord Scarman annd Professor Dworkin share a liberal perspective. Profesor Dworkin's coronation of the judges as the princes of *Law's Empire* is an attractive one for judges to adopt. But it led Lord Scarman, in my view, to the Dworkinian fault of concealing implicit policy options in an explicit discussion of principle. I have usually agreed with his conclusions and marvelled at the glorious language in which the method has been expressed but I think that the methodology is incomplete.

I do not think that Lord Scarman's analysis of the pre-existing law could compare with Lord Reid's or Lord Wilberforce's or Lord Diplock's. That is why some lawyers are reluctant to accord him the highest praise among judges. And, for my part, I regard his analysis of judicial roles as incomplete and his accounts of policy in later cases as virtually non-existent. Nevertheless, I think he can be called a great judge for a variety of reasons which show that our inquiry in this book is only into part of a judge's role. There are other qualities beyond these, such as fact-finding, fairness, impartiality and courtesy within and without court, all of which Lord Scarman possessed in abundance. Moreover, he put them to good use in his various inquiries, and he had a shrewd appreciation of the role of law in society – of the policy factors – to which he gave full rein in what he regarded as the appropriate places such as the Law Commission and the House of Lords as a legislative chamber. Finally, lawyers are wordsmiths and Lord Scarman's prose is compelling, on occasions lilting.

Even someone who is a great judge, however, can err, especially in retirement. Perhaps the lesson of our small sample of famous names from the recent legal past is that they have rarely enhanced their reputations after retirement. They are easy prey for the media, tempting them into injudicious judgments. Former Law Lords never retire, they simply stop reserving their judgment. Lord Scarman's peripheral role in the *Spycatcher* saga, when he wrote to *The Times* criticizing the majority conclusions before they had published their reasons, was surely misguided. His motive, I have suggested, was his deep commitment to the belief that a Bill of Rights would improve the quality of our legal system and our commitment to civil liberties. Yet, as the majority judgments showed, they fully understood the Bill of Rights argument and indeed had applied that form of reasoning to reach their conclusions with which Lord Scarman disagreed. It is appropriate, therefore, to leave the main influence behind the Bill of Rights movement, Lord Scarman, at this point and turn to consider whether incorporating the European Convention on Human Rights into British law would be the best step forward for the role of judges in our society.

Part IV

Changes?

____

22

A Bill of Rights?

So is the way forward for the United Kingdom to enact a Bill of Rights? The question whether we should incorporate the European Convention on Human Rights into our domestic law (which is what is meant by enacting a British Bill of Rights) is not answered by compiling tables of pros and cons. It is a question of attitude, style and emphasis, of political, legal and constitutional culture. One has to grasp the kind of society we would become with the Bill of Rights and then see how that compares with the kind of society we are and the kind we would like to be. I shall therefore focus on another country altogether, drawing on the experience of the USA since theirs is the Constitution most often invoked as the paradigm for those who champion a Bill of Rights. Then I shall try to give the flavour of the European Convention as it presently operates before considering how that would translate to the domestic British context. Finally, I will draw attention to alternative solutions to the perceived problem which the Bill of Rights seeks to address.

Bills of Rights are vague documents. Even tightly drafted laws are susceptible to different interpretations. But Bills of Rights contain such broad statements as 'Everyone has the right to respect for his private life' (Article 8 of the European Convention) which can be applied by judges in diametrically opposed ways. Bills of Rights do not answer all the questions about our civil liberties. Those who interpret the documents have great discretion and therefore power. This was well put by Lord McCluskey in his 1986 Reith Lectures which provided influential support for the view that we should not enact a new Bill of Rights. Lord McCluskey, incidentally, served as Solicitor-General for Scotland under the last Labour Government. He articulates the suspicions of the Left about a Bill of Rights shifting the power from elected politicians to unelected judges. The Right is suspicious of any constitutional change. The Middle is enthusiastic about shifting power since, under the present arrangements, it has none.

My own view is that the debate is misguided. First, we already have a Bill of Rights in the European Convention. Second, it is not a panacea. Third, it is a distraction from the real concern of judging judges. Nevertheless, the debate has captured some imaginations.

So the question, as Humpty Dumpty might have said, is which is to be master – that's all. Are we going to give judges or politicians the last word in defining and developing our rights? Now, superficially, there is some attraction in asking the judges to adopt a greater role, as they do in more or less every other constitution in the world. But, as Lord McCluskey observed, one ought to consider why those countries needed a Bill of Rights. We might be ahead of, not behind, the field. Many Bills of Rights have been introduced as an inadequate recognition of deep problems such as discrimination by new settlers against the original inhabitants of a country. Even countries which have recently thought about adopting a Bill of Rights are not exact analogies. Canada, for example, is a federal country in which a Bill of Rights can help protect the different spheres of influence of the component parts. New Zealand, currently considering a Bill of Rights, does not have a second legislative chamber to check its lower house.

With those warnings in mind, let us nevertheless look at how a Bill of Rights works in another culture, that of the USA. I choose this example since it is widely regarded as the best show-place for a Bill of Rights. By interpreting and applying the US Bill of Rights, the Supreme Court has made some notable strides forward in the establishment, protection and promotion of rights. Perhaps the US example is therefore the best setting in which to understand the way in which a society might resolve contentious issues of civil liberties when it has a Bill of Rights.

Although the US Supreme Court is most often held up as the model for judges acting as interpreters in a Bill of Rights, Lord McCluskey had some doubts in his Reith Lectures:

even the broad, unqualified statements of rights which the Supreme Court Justices have had to apply did not prevent them, until recently, from taking a narrow, legalistic, *laissez-faire* perspective on freedom so as to strike down as unconstitutional legislation designed to stop the exploitation of workers, women, children or immigrants. They legalized slavery; and when it was abolished, they legalized racial segregation. They repeatedly held that women were not entitled to equality with men. They approved the unconstitutional removal by the Executive of the constitutional rights of Americans of Japanese origin after the bombing of Pearl Harbor.

Supporters and doubters both agree that the Supreme Court has enormous power. The court's development of a doctrine of privacy without the right even appearing in the text of the US Bill of Rights is a testimony to that. The path from *Griswold v. Connecticut*, the 1965 case which protected a married couple's right to use contraceptives in the privacy of their bedroom, to *Roe v. Wade*, the 1973 case which protected a woman's decision to abort, has seemed an attractive one to many American liberals. But others have been incensed by the idea that the court has created such a right to privacy out of thin constitutional air. So the important issue is whether one can really approve of the Supreme Court's power independently of liking the latest development. Those who praised the Supreme Court in *Roe v. Wade*, for example, may be changing their minds after the recent 1986 decision in *Bowers, Attorney General of Georgia v. Hardwick*.

In that case, the constitutionality of a Georgia statute which made sodomy a criminal offence was challenged under the right to privacy. The Supreme Court upheld the constitutionality of the statute by 5-4. The majority stressed that they were not judging the wisdom or desirability of the statute but rather its constitutionality. Justice White's majority opinion examined privacy cases such as *Griswold v. Connecticut* and *Roe v. Wade* and concluded:

> we think it evident that none of the rights announced in those cases bears any resemblance to the claimed constitutional right of homosexuals to engage in acts of sodomy, that is asserted in this case. No connection between family,

marriage or procreation on the one hand and homosexual activity on the other has been demonstrated.

This passage rest on two dubious points. The earlier privacy cases are depicted as being about 'family, marriage or procreation'. The instant case is regarded as being about homosexuals. Neither of these crucial assumptions is entirely convincing. *Roe v. Wade*, about an unmarried pregnant woman's wish for an abortion, can only be described as being about family, marriage or procreation in a negative sense. And the Georgia statute at issue in the present case did not distinguish between homosexual and heterosexual activity. The statute made it just as much a criminal offence for a married, heterosexual couple to engage in anal sex as a homosexual couple.

Justice Blackmun, the author of the majority opinion in *Roe v. Wade* (where Justice White and Justice Rehnquist had dissented), this time found himself in the minority. He wrote a vigorous dissent which concluded that:

depriving individuals of the right to choose for themselves how to conduct their intimate relationships poses a far greater threat to the values most deeply rooted in our Nation's history than tolerance or nonconformity could ever do. Because I think the Court today betrays those values, I dissent.

All the judgments in this case deserve an audience on this side of the Atlantic. Between them they encompass many judicial techniques and many varieties of moral judgement. The contrast between majority and minority views of the Constitution is stark and revealing. It suggests that enacting a Bill of Rights does not resolve political disputes. It converts them into a legal form and forum and leaves their resolution up to the chance of who happens to be on the court. This is largely a matter of luck. First, a president may have no opportunity to influence the composition of the court because no judge resigns, retires or dies during his tenure (the Supreme Court Justices have life tenure). Thus President Carter had no occasion to nominate a justice but President Nixon appointed four. Second, even when a president appoints a judge he has no control over the justice's future decisions. Thus the conservative President Eisenhower was wont to say that appointing Chief Justice Warren and Justice Brennan, who were latent liberals, constituted the two most serious mistakes of his presidency.

One case, of course, can hardly be conclusive evidence for or against judicial supremacy in constitutional matters. And perhaps privacy is an atypical right since it nowhere appears explicitly in the text of the constitutional document. It is a wholly judicial development. But if anything is central to the Bill of Rights it is the First Amendment, which protects not only free speech but also the free exercise of religion.

Another 1986 decision of the Supreme Court which therefore merits consideration is *Goldman v. Weinberger*. Goldman was an Orthodox Jew, a rabbi, and a commissioned officer in the US Air Force, serving as a clinical psychologist at a mental health clinic on an Air Force base. He claimed that an Air Force regulation which prohibited the wearing of any headgear indoors infringed his First Amendment freedom to exercise his religious beliefs by wearing a yarmulka. A 5-4 majority decision rejected his claim. Rehnquist J delivered the opinion of the court on behalf of Burger CJ, White, Powell and Stevens JJ. Indignant dissents demonstrated the opposition of Brennan, Marshall, Blackmun and O'Connor JJ.

Justice Rehnquist was prepared to be deferential to the military. But he was so deferential that Justice Brennan, dissenting, described the majority as giving 'credulous deference to unsupported assertions of military necessity'. Thus, Justice Rehnquist was convinced by the military's ploy of asking: whatever next? 'The Government notes that while a yarmulka might not seem obtrusive to a Jew, neither does a turban to a Sikh, a saffron robe to a Satchidananda Ashram – Integral Yogi, nor do dreadlocks to a Rastafarian.' This conjured up a rather implausible picture of the serried ranks of clinical psychologists at air force bases in California going to war in saffron robes or turbans. In the unlikely event that the fighting force's self-image and military discipline depended on Goldman's appearance, he would apparently have undermined his colleagues' morale by wearing a yarmulka but not, presumably, by wearing up to three rings and an identity bracelet, which air force regulations would have allowed.

Again, in reading the majority and the minority opinions, they seem to come from different worlds, or at least different centuries. The personalities and beliefs of the judges are clearly of far greater significance to the outcome of Goldman's case than is the wording of the First Amendment.

Let me illustrate the difference personalities and political convictions can make. The period 1973–4 was the last full term of the Supreme Court which saw both Justice Douglas, the court's leading liberal, and Justice Rehnquist, the leading conservative, sitting together. There were 85 cases on civil rights, which at the risk of over-simplification, we can categorize as disputes between an individual civil libertarian and the state. I am not presuming to comment on the strength of the cases one way or another. But it is striking that in 79 of these 85 cases, Justice Douglas decided for the individual and in only 6 did he agree with the state, whereas Justice Rehnquist supported the state on 69 occasions and the individual on 16. Professor Abraham, one of the leading American constitutional scholars, adds this pertinent observation:

> Yet the two polar opposites heard the same cases, saw the same briefs and other documentation, took the same oath to the same Constitution, were both superbly qualified students and scholars of the law.

Incidentally, the supreme liberal, Douglas, had been confirmed with only 4 votes against him in the Senate in 1939, when he had been described as 'a reactionary tool of Wall Street'! That supports my point about changes in the outlook of the appointee. Rehnquist, one of Nixon's appointments, had more difficulty in securing Senate confirmation, both as an Associate Justice and especially when President Reagan recently nominated him as the new Chief Justice. The Senate Judiciary Committee's hearings in such circumstances deserve examination by those who advocate a British Bill of Rights. In the next chapter we will examine the Bork confirmation battle.

Is this the way forward for the United Kingdom? Problems do not disappear just because a Bill of Rights is enacted. What happens is that judges, who interpret the Bill, take over from politicians as the decision-makers. But who appoints the judges? None other than the politicians in power. So those appointments then become the key step in a presidency. Judges are chosen according to a variety of factors, only one of which is their ability. Their political affiliations, their sex, their race, their religion, their friendship with the President, their geographical origins, can all outweigh any deficiencies in their legal or judicial talents. Although President Reagan will be remembered for appointing the first woman Justice in the history of the Supreme Court, 92 per cent of his appointments to the federal bench have been male: 98 per cent white and 98 per cent Republican.

A couple of 5–4 split decisions in the US Supreme Court do not detract from the glorious, unanimous decision in *Brown*, which I have already described as a model judgment, nor from the Supreme Court's role in the American Constitution. But they do remind us that those who interpret a Bill of Rights have great power which they can exercise in a variety of ways, not all of which will be to our liking. As the United Kingdom approaches the tercentennial celebrations of its own limited Bill of Rights, those who argue that we should incorporate the European Convention into our domestic law and thus adopt a new Bill of Rights, must focus on who will interpret and apply the general language of that document.

One decision of the European Court of Human Rights stands out in the armoury of those who demand that we incorporate the Convention into our domestic law. Time after time, reference is made to the *Sunday Times Thalidomide* case, where the European Court ruled in 1979 that the English law of contempt of court, as laid down by the House of Lords in the 1974 case *Attorney General v. Times Newspapers*, was in contravention of Article 10's guarantee of freedom of expression. This finally freed the *Sunday Times* to publish an article which was critical of Distillers, the manufacturers of the drug Thalidomide. Although the European Court's ruling vindicated the newspaper's fight to publish, it came several years too late, of course, to affect the actual dispute between Distillers and the families affected by Thalidomide. Supporters of incorporation praise the European Court for this critique of the English law and only bemoan the delay involved in taking a case such as this to Strasbourg. If we had had an incorporated Bill of Rights, they argue, English courts could have made that decision. But would they have done so? The Law Lords had considerable discretion as it was when they made their 1974 decision which the European Court criticized. Moreover, in a subsequent case, the House of Lords' majority repeated its restrictive approach, notwithstanding the European Court's decision. Statute law subsequently introduced the Strasbourg ruling into the domestic law.

But we should not get carried away by this example of a liberal decision by the European Court. We must bear in mind that it was made by the narrowest of margins. The European Court split 11-9. Nine European judges, then, were prepared to interpret the Convention so as to allow the Law Lords' decision to stand. The structure of the relevant Article is typical of the Convention's drafting and revealing of the latitude allowed to the interpreters:

> Article 10
> (1) Everyone has the right to freedom of expression. The right shall include freedom to hold opinions and to receive and impart information and ideas without interference by public authority and regardless of frontiers. This Article shall not prevent States from requiring the licensing of broadcasting, television or cinema enterprises.
> (2) The exercise of these freedoms, since it carries with it duties and responsibilities, may be subject to such formalities, conditions and restrictions or penalties as are prescribed by law and are necessary in a democratic society, in the interests of national security, territorial integrity or public safety, for the prevention of disorder or crime, for the protection of health or morals, for the protection of the reputation or rights of others, for preventing the disclosure of information received in confidence, or for maintaining the authority and impartiality of the judiciary.

Incorporating such an article into British law is not going to resolve anything in itself. Just like the 11 in the majority or the 9 in the minority, the interpreter has a broad discretion as to how to balance the right against its many broad exceptions. Politicians and judges already make this kind of decision, albeit without perhaps explicitly acknowledging the trade-off. The important issues are who has the decisive say and how can they be influenced. If Members of Parliament have the major role, at least they are exposed to the pressure of the media, the lobbyists, the interest groups and, most importantly, at least they are removable by the electorate. Moreover, they will often have the benefit of official reports and a great deal of briefing from departments, parties and unofficial researchers. Judges, in contrast, are deliberately insulated from pressure, are irremovable and decide on the very limited basis of what counsel for two parties in a particular dispute care to put before them. On this occasion, our natural sympathies are with those who suffered through Thalidomide and with the campaigning newspaper, so the bare majority of the European Court came to what we would regard as the 'right' decision. It is understandable but hasty to claim that the European Convention is *therefore* a most desirable domestic Bill of Rights. For if one's only justification is that the European Court here achieved the 'right' balance, what if it sometimes gets the 'wrong' result, or if British judges would get the 'wrong' result?

In order to see how the Convention is being interpreted today, let us consider three European cases which received some publicity in the British press in 1987. These three applications of the European Convention concerned: a transsexual's right to privacy; Irish citizens' right to remarry; and trade unionists' right to freedom of association.

What exactly does it mean, for example, to say that we have a right to respect for our private lives, as in Article 8 of the European Convention? The Article runs as follows:

(1) Everyone has the right to respect for his private and family life, his home and his correspondence.
(2) There shall be no interference by a public authority with the exercise of this right except such as is in accordance with the law and is necessary in a democratic society in the interests of national security, public safety or the economic well-being of the country, for the prevention of disorder or crime, for the protection of health or morals, or for protection of the rights and freedoms of others.

The question in the recent Rees case was whether a transsexual's right to privacy was breached by the refusal of the Registrar

General to amend the transsexual's birth certificate. How would you interpret and apply Article 8 to this problem? There was considerable disagreement among the European institutions. The European Commission on Human Rights unanimously felt that Rees's right to privacy had been violated. But then the European Court of Human Rights, by 12 votes to 3, decided that the Commission was wrong and that Article 8 had not been breached. If the commission and the court are in such disagreement, perhaps we can conclude that privacy seems to be a controversial right. Bills of Rights do not answer all the questions. Those who interpret the documents have great discretion and therefore power. How a British court would interpret that right to privacy is anyone's guess.

What about the absence of provision for divorce under Irish law? Does that contravene Article 8, set out above, or Article 12? The latter Article reads: 'Men and women of marriageable age have the right to marry and to found a family, according to the national laws governing the exercise of this right.' In *Johnston v. Ireland*, the court dealt with a man who was formally separated from his wife and had been living with another woman for fifteen years. The Irish Constitution prohibited divorce so he was unable to divorce his wife in order to marry the woman with whom he now lived and with whom he had had a child. Again, how would you interpret Articles 8 and 12? The European Court, by 16 votes to 1, decided that Ireland's ban on divorce did not violate the Convention.

Our third example is the European Commission on Human Rights' consideration of the ban on trade unions at the Government Communications Headquarters in Cheltenham. When the Law Lords decided that Mrs Thatcher was entitled to ban the unions without consultation since she felt national security would be imperilled by negotiation, it was claimed in some quarters that this was the kind of case which would be decided differently if we had a Bill of Rights. Similarly, there have been many misplaced expressions of confidence that the 'Zircon' raid of the BBC by the police would have been condemned by judges interpreting a Bill of Rights. Yet there is little reason to suppose that judges who defer to claims of national security as in the Law Lords' decision or in the granting of the 'Zircon' warrant, would somehow intervene more readily under the umbrella of a Bill of Rights. For national security is an exception to the rights contained in the Convention.

Sure enough, the European Commission rejected the GCHQ unions' claim that the ban on trade union membership at GCHQ violated their right under Article 11 of the Convention. Thus the unions' case did not even reach the European Court since it could not pass the first stage of convincing the Commission that there was a case to answer.

Lord Jowitt, then the Lord Chancellor, described the Convention at the time of accepting it in 1950 as 'so vague and woolly that it may mean almost anything'. To be more precise it will mean whatever its interpreters want it to mean. Of course, whether or not we have a domestic Bill of Rights, we will still be subject to the European institutions' interpretation of the Convention. But the court does tend to allow what it calls a 'margin of appreciation' to national laws, so it is vital to decide whether the final word on the domestic interpretation should come from Parliament or the courts. Even an unentrenched domestic Bill of Rights would, in practice, shift that power away from Parliament (which would be reluctant to be seen to be legislating 'contrary to the Bill or Rights' even if it technically could do so) and towards the judges. Is that really desirable?

It could be argued that we already defer to the European Court of Human Rights, so should we not allow British judges the same power to review our law in the light of the Convention, instead of suffering the allegedly humiliating spectacle of washing our dirty linen in public at Strasbourg? This argument, often put forward by the tumble-drying classes who have no idea of washing laundry in public, is flawed. The origin of the European Convention was the idea of the Western European democracies watching each other in front of the public of Europe to guard against a repeat of fascism's abuses of human rights. Anyone who watches *EastEnders* will know that the launderette is a place not only to wash dirty linen but also to exchange ideas. It is central to the development of community values.

But is the analogy with European judges really apt? There is a big difference between twenty-one European judges, one from each country, interpreting a vague document and one, three or five British judges having the same power. This is not a criticism of our own judges. It is, rather, an acknowledgement of two facts. First, the full European Court brings a breadth of experience and a variety of traditions which cannot be matched by a small group of British judges.

Second, no single, transient government can turn a majority of the European Court. But any one government can and usually does influence the make-up of our own judiciary. Lord Hailsham, the Lord Chancellor, and Mrs Thatcher have nominated all the senior judges bar one during the period since 1979. They have done that without seeking to shift the courts significantly to the right. But could they, or any other government, be so self-effacing if judges were yet more powerful? Would we not expect that the more powerful the courts become, the more pressure there would be to appoint sympathetic judges? As the American experience shows, this does not always work to the satisfaction of those who appoint. Judges sometimes confound the expectations of those who choose them. But we would inevitably slide down the road to American-style nominations, based on political ideology, and confirmation hearings. Is that the route we want to travel?

The trouble with enacting a Bill of Rights, therefore, is that it sets us on an uncertain constitutional path. It might lead to great gains in our civil liberties. But it might not. It will certainly alter the nature of appointments to the judiciary. It may well be that this is a much-needed development, but we need to know what the new system of appointing judges would be. The corollary of a Bill of Rights ought to be a Minister of Justice in the Commons who would have to account to a Select Committee for his nominations to the Bench. Unless this comes hand in glove with a Bill of Rights, there is the danger that future appointments to the Bench will be based on party political views without any control machinery.

Moreover, irrespective of questions about the judges, it is difficult to believe that British court procedure is the best environment for a thorough analysis of such problematic political questions as the Bill would give them. Why should an adversarial dispute between two parties, largely argued on the basis of precedent, be the ideal forum in which to decide, for instance, whether a Labour government's proposals against private education or in favour of re-nationalization offend the First Protocol to the European Convention?

We are indeed a long way off the kind of procedure which Americans and others would associate with courts interpreting a Bill of Rights. We have not yet mastered the art of lawyers filing briefs as *amici curiae*, 'friends of the court'. We have not yet mastered the idea of Brandeis briefs, in which a full range of social and economic evidence about the likely consequences of alternative judicial conclusions is put to the judges. We have not yet adopted the American practice of assigning the best young lawyers to act as clerks, or research assistants, to the judges. We have not yet used the European Economic Community's equivalent of using more experienced lawyers to act as *referendaires* to the European Court of Justice (a different entity from the European Court of Human Rights, the former applies Community law in Luxembourg, the latter Convention law in Strasbourg). Of course, one might expect some of these developments to emerge once we had a Bill of Rights but it would be more reassuring if we were shown, in advance, some commitment by the legal professions to reform of our court procedures in order to fulfil different and broader duties.

If, contrary to my argument, judges are to pull the constitutional strings in the future, we should hasten to prepare lawyers for that wide-ranging task. We will have to shake up our court procedure. And we will have to think seriously about the qualifications for judicial service. Judge Learned Hand, the eminent American lawyer who was sadly denied the chance to grace the Supreme Court himself, explained the formidable task in terms which demonstrate the magnitude and latitude of the task we would be assigning to judges:

> I venture to believe that it is as important to a judge called upon to pass on a question of constitutional law, to have a bowing acquaintance with Acton and Maitland, with Thucydides, Gibbon, and Carlyle, with Homer, Dante, Shakespeare, and Milton, with Machiavelli, Montaigne, and Rabelais, with Plato, Bacon, Hume and Kant as with books that have been specifically written on the subject. For in such matters everything turns upon the spirit in which he

approaches the question before him. The words he must construe are empty vessels into which he can pour nearly everything he will. Men do not gather figs of thistles, nor supply institutions from judges whose outlook is limited by parish or class. They must be aware that there are before them more than verbal problems; more than final solutions cast in generalizations of universal applicability. They must be aware of the changing social tensions in every society which make it an organism; which demand new schemata of adaptation; which will disrupt it, if rigidly confined.

Those who argue that such a job description indicates the enormous power of judges who act as constitutional guardians might well put their faith instead in those who exercise ultimate power in society being removable through elections and accountable through public argument. In British practice, this means politicians not judges. Thus the Leftish argument against a Bill of Rights is, in essence, that politics is about power, that this should not be obscured by legal form, and that the power should not be exercised by irremovable, unaccountable judges. That is not a complacent argument. On the contrary, it demands reform of a different kind. As Professor John Griffith has argued:

> I believe firmly that political decisions should be taken by politicians. In a society like ours this means by people who are removable. It is an obvious corollary of this that the responsibility and accountability of our rulers should be real and not fictitious. And of course our existing institutions, especially the House of Commons, need strengthening. And we need to force governments out into the open. So also the freedom of the Press should be enlarged by the amendment of laws which restrict discussion.

Judges are not the only possible interpreters of a Bill of Rights. If we have enough imagination to challenge the existing constitutional order, why stop at introducing broad guarantees of rights? Let's think seriously about the guardians of such rights.

Should we entrust such power to unelected lawyers, however distinguished in their own profession? Or should we opt for a Constitutional Committee of the Privy Council which would have a broader composition, perhaps along the lines of the French Conseil Constitutionnel?

In a Fabian paper in 1968, Anthony Lester QC began the movement for a new British Bill of Rights by calling for the incorporation of the European Convention on Human Rights, but at that time he favoured making it unenforceable in the courts. Although he now supports the enforcement of a Bill of Rights through the courts, he then thought that instead of transferring power to judges, we should create a Constitutional Council which could make recommendations to Parliament about the compatibility with the Bill of Rights of legislative or executive action (or I would add, legislative or executive inaction and the inadequacies of the common law). I would suggest a Constitutional Committee of the Privy Council, consisting of not only the senior judges but also senior politicians and perhaps augmented by the kind of people who head Royal Commissions and Committees of Inquiry (Williams, Warnock, Blake, Bullock, Quinton) and also some wise people from a broader background, some who do not share the Great and Good's role of heading Oxbridge colleges.

Such a body could be modelled on the French Conseil Constitutionnel. It would have certain advantages over a court, namely a broader composition, the opportunity to consider matters in advance, and surmounting the objections of opponents that any such Bill will have indeterminable, and possibly harmful, consequences for the judiciary. The idea of a Constitutional Council would fit in well with the Law Commission and the increasingly impressive system of Select Committees. It would not be a barrier to the eventual decision to make the Convention directly enforceable. Indeed, it could usefully examine the ramifications of creating a Constitutional Court. If the real motive for the Bill of Rights movement is the promotion of human rights and the real motive for objection is the danger of yet more politicization of the judiciary, then surely a Constitutional Council deserves serious consideration by both sides. It is not enough to campaign for a Bill of Rights without answering the objections. It is not enough to object without providing another answer to those who question the protection of civil liberties under current arrangements.

Nor is it enough to expect any constitutional reordering to safeguard our rights on its own. As the Weimar Republic showed, a perfect paper constitution is not an adequate protection of civil liberties. Indeed, it is an impoverished vision of the human condition which thinks only of changing institutions and laws. We best protect rights by changing attitudes.

We have already acknowledged the initial Left-ish argument that politics, including claims for rights, rest on power. Now we have to respect the Right-ish argument that we need to conserve our cultural scepticism of those in power, we need to develop our personal responsibility for civil liberties, we cannot regard a Bill of Rights as much more than a diversion from the real safeguard for our liberties. The price of liberty, as Curran's aphorism reminds us, is eternal vigilance.

Just as the Right could agree with the Left on the need to have power where we can see it and exercise some control over it, so the Left could agree with the Right on this final point that attitudes are more important than legal form. Thus the point was well put by that liberal judge on whose wisdom we have already relied, Learned Hand:

> I often wonder whether we do not rest our hopes too much upon constitutions, upon laws and upon courts. These are false hopes; believe me, these are false hopes. Liberty lies in the hearts of men and women; when it dies there no constitution, no law, no court can save it; no constitution, no law, no court can even do much to help it. While it lies there it needs no constitution, no law, no court to save it.

Finally, the same message was well put by Professor Grant Gilmore who concluded his summary of *The Ages of American Law* with a note of caution. Undoubtedly, the US Bill of Rights has recently been used to good effect, particularly the 'due process' clause of its 14th Amendment. But even its greatest supporters would echo Learned Hand's warning. Thus Professor Gilmore leaves us with the following speculation: 'In Heaven there will be no law, and the lion will lie down with the lamb . . . In Hell there will be nothing but law, and due process will be meticulously observed.'

I would merely add that the path to Hell is paved with good

intentions, such as the good faith of those who argue for a British Bill of Rights. I do not claim that such a development would lead us down the road to Hell but neither do I believe that a Bill of Rights would take us straight to Heaven. I suspect the less glamorous truth to be that the way forward for those who value civil liberties involves a lot of hard work in Purgatory.

Bork – Supreme Injustice?

Whether or not we enact a Bill of Rights in the United Kingdom, we must think seriously about the appointment of judges. In this regard, the experience of the USA will prove invaluable. The year 1987 saw a remarkable battle when President Reagan attempted to put Judge Robert Bork on the Supreme Court. The ensuing controversy needs to be studied on this side of the Atlantic for the glimpse of a possible future, desired by some yet despised by others, for the judging of judges.

The Senate Judiciary Committee, chaired by Joseph Biden who was at the time a Democrat presidential candidate, began its hearings on Judge Bork just as the USA celebrated the bicentenary of its Constitution, signed on 17 September 1787. The hearings amounted to a national seminar on how to judge judges, or how not to judge judges, depending on one's perspective. The Committee recommended that the Senate should refuse to confirm Bork and the full Senate took that advice in voting 58–42 to reject him.

President Reagan was elected partly to select conservative judges and there is no doubt that the defeat of Judge Bork was a major rebuff for him. It might influence the 1988 presidential campaign since the next president will undoubtedly have the opportunity to nominate successors to the three liberal musketeers, Justices Brennan, Marshall and Blackmun, who are all in or reaching their eighties. That will, in turn, confirm the ideology of the Supreme Court for the rest of the century and well beyond.

The defeat of Judge Bork might also influence the way in which other potential Justices behave. It might even affect the way in which the present Supreme Court behaves. We need to consider the Bork saga for its own sake and also to see whether its influences will extend across the Atlantic.

President Reagan had not encountered opposition to his two previous nominees to the court. There were three reasons, in addition to her merit, which immunised his first candidate from hostile reaction. When he nominated Sandra Day O'Connor, her status as the first woman Justice deflected attention from her political views, the court had a liberal majority despite her promotion, and both the President and the Senate were conservative and elected on a platform of appointing conservative judges. Reagan's second nominee, Antonin Scalia, also avoided controversy for similar reasons, again in addition to his talents. He was the first Italian-American to be nominated to the court in a country which places great store on ethnic origins, he was replacing Chief Justice Burger who was himself conservative, and he again faced a Republican Senate.

By 1987, however, the rules of the game had changed. The liberals and the conservatives now numbered four each on the court and Bork was nominated to replace the centrist, swing-voter, Justice Lewis Powell. His choice therefore became critical. Control of the Senate had also changed hands in the 1986 elections, so that the Democrats now had a majority and could therefore mount a real challenge to a Reagan nominee.

Moreover, Bork was a controversial figure, being the man who followed President Nixon's orders to fire Archibald Cox, the Watergate Special Prosecutor, when his two senior colleagues in the Attorney General's Justice Department resigned rather than obey the presidential instruction. By nominating Bork and exposing him to an aggressive Senate Judiciary Committee, Reagan resuscitated the Watergate story just when the Irangate controversy was fading from public attention.

Bork was, above all, controversial because of his judicial philosophy and his hostility to some Supreme Court decisions, which he would have been in a position to change if he had been confirmed. Bork thinks that the judges should only interpret the Constitution according to the 'original intent' of the framers. This seemed to bode ill for the doctrine of privacy which is nowhere explicitly mentioned in the Constitution. When judges have gone beyond the 'original intent' Bork believes that the 'Court ought always to be open to rethink constitutional problems'. Putting those two views together, he thinks that the 1973 pro-abortion decision, *Roe v.*

Wade, based on the alleged right to privacy, is wrong. As he put it to the Senate Committee when he was earlier nominated to the federal bench (and confirmed without dissent), 'I am convinced, as I think most scholars are, that *Roe v. Wade* is, itself, an unconstitutional decision, a serious and wholly unjustifiable usurpation of state legislative authority.' The 7–2 majority for *Roe v. Wade* in 1973 was whittled down to a 5–4 majority in an abortion decision in 1986 when Powell, whom Bork was nominated to replace, was one of that slender majority. Bork's nomination was perceived as critical to how another abortion case, already scheduled for the next Supreme Court term, would be decided.

Discomfiting Bork, a former Yale Law School professor, should not have been possible on grounds of intellect. Whereas one of Nixon's unsuccessful nominations, Carswell, was such a weak lawyer that even his chief supporter in the Senate could only argue, 'so what if he is mediocre, there are a lot of mediocre people out there who need representation', Bork is anything but mediocre. Nevertheless, and in addition to Watergate, his forthright views were dredged up to haunt him. Most seriously he once wrote in a 1963 magazine article that a proposed federal civil rights law which aimed to prevent restaurant owners from excluding blacks was an unjustifiable limitation on the freedom of whites to choose with whom to do business. His explanation was that he has changed his mind and many a Supreme Court judge has come away from that kind of statement in his past to become enlightened. Most famously, the impeccably liberal Supreme Court Justice Hugo Black had been forced to admit, just after his confirmation in 1937, the truth of newspaper reports about his membership of the racist Klu Klux Klan in the mid-1920s.

When William Rehnquist (already an Associate Justice on the Court) was nominated as Chief Justice by Reagan in 1986, he was quizzed in the Judiciary Committee on three damaging allegations – that as clerk to a Supreme Court Justice in the 1950s he wrote a memorandum arguing against the celebrated decision in *Brown* to order desegregation of the schools; that he bought and sold houses with restrictive covenants against Jews; and that he harassed black voters in the 1960s. Rehnquist denied that the memo reflected his own views, he denied that he had ever scrutinized the minute details of his house deals and he denied that he had harassed voters.

But in each case, further information had emerged since his first nomination hearing and Bork too received a far tougher ride than when he was first made a judge. Even since the Rehnquist and Scalia hearings in 1986, there had been significant changes which pointed to a tougher examination. Not only had the Democrats taken control of the Senate majority and therefore of the Judiciary Committee but also President Reagan's personal prestige was at a low ebb in the wake of the Iran–Contra hearings.

Yet another ingredient which promised a real battle was that in addition to Edward Kennedy, a forthright opponent of Reagan nominees, at least two presidential candidates, the chairman Senator Joe Biden and Senator Paul Simon, were on the Judiciary Committee. They needed to judge their judging of the judge to perfection, not to let Bork off lightly but not to push too far. The US nation was watching their performance, as much as Bork's, at least on news highlights and, if they so wished, continuously on cable. As the country celebrated the bicentenary of its Constitution in the spotlight of television, these senators made their play for the presidency. Biden was the first casualty, the spotlight falling on him just as he chose to plagiarize a speech by Neil Kinnock in establishing his humble background. Biden was pressed by the press and withdrew from the presidential race. Bork, of course, was the more important casualty.

It was not clear how far the senators could go in embarrassing Bork. In particular, one of the unresolved questions of two hundred years of the USA's Constitution was whether the Senate would be justified in rejecting a presidential nomination because the Senate disagreed with the judge's ideology. Some 20 per cent of nominees have been rejected over the two centuries and some of those have undoubtedly suffered because of their political views. George Washington, for example, found his nominee for Chief Justice, John Rutledge, rejected because of his opposition to the Jay Treaty with our country.

Even trickier unresolved questions would have flooded on to the American political marketplace if Bork had been confirmed. The thrust of Bork's judicial philosophy is to remit difficult questions of social policy to the elected representatives of the people, especially through the state legislatures. Yet while many criticize Supreme Court decisions of which they disappove, they perhaps also find it easier that the court has in recent decades made moral decisions on behalf of the nation, providing a shield behind which politicians can hide by claiming that while they think one thing, they have to defer to the Supreme Court which thinks the opposite. The coincidence of the Bork hearings, the forthcoming presidential election and the Bicentenary forced the American public to face a vital question after two hundred years of varying experience: does it wish to be ruled by 'a bevy of Platonic Guardians', as the Supreme Court has been described, or do the People intend to take more responsibility for their own liberties?

But while that fits in with our debates on whether or not to enact an American-style Bill of Rights, my concern in this chapter is to stress that Americans have gone a lot further (some would say too far) in judging judges. This is mostly because of the Bill of Rights and the importance which the Supreme Court has in the US Constitution. But there is no doubting that the judging of judges is a multi-million-dollar industry in itself and is widely regarded in the USA as *essential* to judging judges.

How is this an industry? The Bill of Rights leads Americans to favour single-issue pressure groups which mount court campaigns –most famously in the case of the 1954 decision to end racial segregation in the schools – to achieve political aims. These groups realize the vital importance of who decides such cases and therefore spend a lot of time and money on researching potential candidates to see if their views fit and, if not, whether there is any damaging information which could be used to prevent the nomination or its confirmation. There are also associations which are interested simply in enhancing the reputation of the court, so that the American Bar Association, in particular, launches extensive inquiries of every nominee. In the ABA's Scalia testimony, for example, it based its enthusiastic recommendation for confirmation on interviews with 340 people, including 200 judges and all the Supreme Court Justices; the ABA Committee interviewed 60 leading professors of constitutional law and commissioned two studies of all Scalia's opinions. This is their standard practice for all nominations to the Supreme Court.

Meanwhile, back in the UK, where is the opportunity to voice concerns about a judge before appointment or promotion?

Nowhere. The matter is jealously guarded by the Lord Chancellor's Department despite pressure to bring it into the comparatively open spaces of a Parliamentary Select Committee.

Of course, the judges usually survive this scrutiny, so one might question its effectiveness. But 20 per cent of nominees are rejected and, more importantly, presidents are discouraged from proposing candidates who might fall at this hurdle. Moreover, the knowledge that one will have to submit oneself to such public examination might affect the way in which judges behave earlier in their careers. Again, of course one could argue that this has its bad points and I am not in favour of appointments to the British judiciary based on political ideology. I merely draw to readers' attention the fact that the most significant lesson to learn from the USA is not the obvious one that a Bill of Rights gives judges power but the concomitant point that we need to think seriously about how to check such power.

The rejection of Judge Bork raises many issues, indeed many mysteries. One mystery for non-Americans is how Justice Antonin Scalia came to be confirmed unanimously by the Senate when Bork, with whom he sided in 84 out of their 86 joint decisions on the same court, was rejected by 58–42. Of the two cases in which they disagreed, one has become legendary in that Scalia launched a ferocious attack on Bork for being too *liberal* in his interpretation of the First Amendment. Senator Biden said, in voting for Scalia, 'notwithstanding the nominee's conservative bent, there is no indication that the nominee's philosophy would unravel the settled fabric of constitutional law'. Senator Kennedy said, in also voting for Scalia, that, 'I too find that Judge Scalia is in the mainstream of thought of our society.'

Another curiosity is how Bork came to be confirmed unanimously to that Court of Appeals in 1982 but rejected for the Supreme Court in 1987. The *New York Times*, which led the opposition to Bork this time round, had hailed him as a natural choice when he faced the Senate Judiciary Committee five years earlier on being nominated to the federal bench:

Bork . . . is a legal scholar of distinction and principle . . . One may differ heatedly from him on specific issues like abortion, but those are differences of philosophy, not principle. Differences of philosophy are what the 1980 election was about; Robert Bork is, given President Reagan's philosophy, a natural choice for an important judicial vacancy.

What had changed? As we shall see in the next paragraph, Bork's record on the Court of Appeals reinforced this estimation of his talents. Yet by 1987 the *New York Times* was urging Bork's rejection.

A further oddity, then, is how Bork could be described as outside the mainstream of American jurisprudence when *none* of his 400 or more decisions on the Court of Appeals had been overturned by the Supreme Court. Indeed, although Judge Bork was in the majority in 95 per cent of the cases he decided, which itself suggests that he is within the mainstream of judicial philosophy, when he dissented and the Supreme Court reviewed the case he was vindicated, and the Court of Appeals majority defeated, every time.

I am by no means an apologist for Bork. On the contrary, I chose not to take a course with him when I had the opportunity to do so as a graduate student at Yale Law School in 1979–80. Moreover, I think his judicial philosophy is nonsensical in its extreme form. But beneath the hysteria, and beneath my own political differences with him, I have some sympathy for the man who was unfairly pilloried. The reality is that judges are more or less running for office in the USA. Political acceptability is the name of the game. Should we endorse that in this country? A closer look at the confirmation, or in this case rejection, process is necessary.

In particular, what intrigues me is that one of the ringleaders of the anti-Bork brigade was none other than Ronald Dworkin. Dworkin has now written three biting attacks on Bork, one in 1984 when he feared that Bork would be nominated by Reagan to the Supreme Court, another in the summer of 1987 when he was, and the third in the winter of 1987 after he had been rejected. All three appeared in the *New York Review of Books*. They attracted much criticism but remained influential. The almost personal nature of these articles led many people to wonder what was happening. Professor M.B.E. Smith was moved, after the second attack, to write a long, indignant and convincing letter to the *NYBR* which began thus:

> Professor Ronald Dworkin has twice in your pages launched an extraordinary attack upon Judge Bork, depicting him as a right-wing ideologue who uses an 'original intent' constitutional theory as a mere mask for lawless judging. But Bork's judicial practice is wholly consistent with Dworkin's jurisprudential theory . . . Hence it appears that Dworkin's real complaint is simply that he disagrees with Bork on controversial questions of constitutional right.

Dworkin was at the intellectual end of a multi-million-dollar campaign against Bork. A rainbow coalition of liberal groups spent the summer and fall of 1987 researching, investigating and lobbying. The anti-intellectual end of the rainbow came with the television commercials, paid for by People for the American Way, in which Gregory Peck criticized Judge Bork, claiming that, 'He defended poll taxes and literacy tests which kept many Americans from voting. He opposed the civil rights law that ended "whites only" signs at lunch counters. He doesn't believe the Constitution protects your right to privacy.'

Even Dworkin found this a little hard to take: 'the Peck commercial was indeed misleading in several respects.' A footnote summarizes Dworkin's estimation of the commercial:

> The Peck advertisement made four claims about Bork's record. It said that he 'defended poll taxes and literacy tests' which suggests that he approved these devices for keeping people from voting; in fact Bork argued only that the Constitution did not make the devices unconstitutional. It said he opposed the civil rights laws (as he did, in 1963) but failed to add that he has changed his mind since. It said he thinks that free speech does not apply to art, literature, and music; without adding that, though he took that position without qualification in 1971, he recently said that freedom of speech does hold for the arts because, as he had not recognized then, the arts have a bearing on politics. It said, finally, that he 'doesn't believe the Constitution protects your rights to privacy,' which is true, and, on the evidence of

the hearings, the single most convincing charge the advertisement made.

I am not so sure as Dworkin that this last allegation was true. If I may quote what Bork actually said in his confirmation hearings:

> No civilized person wants to live in a society without a lot of privacy in it. And the Framers of the Constitution protected privacy in a variety of ways. The First Amendment protects free exercise of religion. The free speech provision of the First Amendment has been held to protect the privacy of membership lists and a person's associations in order to make the free speech right effective. The Fourth Amendment protects the individual's home and office from unreasonable searches and seizures. It usually requires a warrant. The Fifth Amendment has a right against self-incrimination. There's much more. There's a lot of privacy in the Constitution.

What Bork objects to is a 'generalized right of privacy. Suppose a senator introduced a bill that said every man, woman and child in this country has a right of privacy. I don't think that bill would go anywhere until he told everybody exactly what the right of privacy protected. Did it protect incest? Did it protect beating your wife in private?'

It was indeed a Bork judgment on the right of a homosexual navy officer to privacy which particularly annoyed Dworkin and which he attacked in his first criticism of Bork in the *New York Review of Books*. Yet the Supreme Court subsequently endorsed the Bork approach, in effect, in its majority decision in *Bowers, Attorney General of Georgia v. Hardwick*. Now I have criticized that interpretation of the privacy doctrine. I would prefer Dworkin's view to Bork's but I would admit that I am preferring one political view to another. I disagree with Bork's vision of privacy but I disagree with Dworkin's assumption that there is one right answer to privacy questions which is somehow inherent in the Constitution.

Whatever the merits of the privacy debate, my point here is that the advertising *was* misleading. But Dworkin has some better points to make in claiming that the advertising *for* Bork was equally unfair and that Bork's unimpressive personal performance at the hearings was more important than the claims of his opponents in losing him support.

Before proceeding to that point, on which I agree with Dworkin, I should add that the Peck advertisement was not an isolated case. The pressure group People for the American Way ran newspaper advertisements, under the heading 'Robert Bork vs. the People', this time claiming that he stood for 'sterilizing workers', 'no privacy' and perhaps an agenda to 'turn back the clock on civil rights'. The National Abortion Rights Action League's advertisement also warned that Bork might try 'to wipe out every advance women have made in the twentieth century'.

Notwithstanding these attacks, I am sure that Bork could have overcome the hostile groups if he had made a good impression on television during his lengthy hearings before the Senate Judiciary Committee. Bork testified for 32 hours personally before the Judiciary Committee, which also heard 62 witnesses speak for him and 48 against him. Dworkin rightly observed that 'Bork seemed too dry and academic and lacking in charm' and rightly observed that that is not a particularly good reason for rejecting him. Even Bork's personal appearance apparently lost him votes. Senator Howell Heflin asked Bork to explain his beard. Bork blamed a sabbatical in England and a week-long canal-boat-trip. The boat's sink was right against a wall and so Bork would have had to shave with his left hand, which he was unable to do. The mind boggles at British judges being asked about their appearance. Although Lord Goff's moustache is more distinguished than Judge Bork's wispy beard, I cannot imagine his being called to account for it. Senator Heflin was satisfied with the explanation for the beard, concluding that, 'There's nothing wrong with it because there are a lot of bearded voters out there that I don't want to make mad.'

There were, of course, many more serious questions and many more serious reasons for Bork's failure. In particular, Bork suffered for appearing to undergo what Dworkin calls a 'confirmation conversion'. He seemed to shift his ground in order to appease his critics rather than defending his established views without reservation.

One of the most interesting objections to Bork revealed by the confirmation process was the opposition signed by some 1,925 law school professors, some 40 per cent of the academic lawyers in the USA. But in the world of *realpolitik*, the most telling criticisms came from others. Senators were left in no doubt that black Americans distrusted Bork. Indeed, Bork himself told one Senator that, 'My greatest disappointment is not in losing. It is that black Americans believe I am a racist, and that hurts me, hurts me deeply.' The most damaging individual criticism perhaps came from former President Jimmy Carter. Although Bork was introduced by former President Gerald Ford and was supported by former Chief Justice Warren Burger and Carter's counsel, Lloyd Cutler, Jimmy Carter's letter to the Committee Chairman was a devastating riposte. He noted that 'some prominent lawyers who served in my administration' had testified for Bork. He then explained his own, contrary, views:

> Just to avoid any misunderstanding, I would like for the members of your committee to know that I am strongly opposed to Judge Bork's confirmation. I find many of his forcefully expressed opinions in contradiction to my concept of what this nation is and ought to be . . . As a Southerner who has observed personally the long and difficult years of the struggle for civil rights for black and other minority people, I find Judge Bork's impressively consistent opinions to be particularly obnoxious.

How did the black objections to Bork carry so much weight? Senator Breaux of Louisiana, for example, was elected by 90 per cent of the black vote in his state but only 40 per cent of the white vote in 1986. As he observed:

> Those who helped us get elected – the black voters, the working people – are united in their opposition to Bork, and don't think for a moment that we are going to ignore that . . .
> If you vote against Bork, those in favor of him will be mad at you for a week. But if you vote for him, those who don't like him will be mad at you for the rest of their lives.

For all the politicking, there remains the basic jurisprudential dispute which is at the heart of this book and which determined Bork's fate. Judge Bork is the most intellectually distinguished proponent of an intellectually undistinguished theory of adjudication, sometimes dubbed 'original intent', sometimes 'historicism'. According to Dworkin, this view 'insists that the Constitution creates no rights except those explicitly in the text of the document, interpreted to express some pertinent expectation of the framers'.

Dworkin is quite right to expose the inadequacies of this approach. There may not be one, or any, original intent of the framers which helps resolve the current problem. And if there is any such thing as original intent, then it seems that the framers intended that their own interpretations of their constitutional provisions should *not* bind future courts. The doctrine of original intent is a device by which the judge can reach conservative conclusions under the cover of what the framers wanted. Mind you, I regard Dworkin's theory of adjudication as another cover, this time for reaching liberal conclusions. Indeed, there is some sense in saying that Dworkin is arguing for the most original intent of them all and that that has as little substance as any other original intent.

Original intent, then, is dead as a judicial doctrine. That is the result of the Bork hearings and it is one which I applaud. My criticism of original intent is that although it makes an effort to address my first and third questions, it pretends to ignore the second (evaluating the consequences of a judicial decision) and gives unsophisticated answers to the questions which it does try to answer. That is my objection to Dworkin's theory as well. I do not believe that Bork or Dworkin are indifferent to the results of their interpretations of the law. I am sure that they have that in mind but they refuse to acknowledge it. Indeed, Dworkin is more guilty of this than is Bork. I am unaware of *any* admission by Dworkin that *any* case whose results conflict with his political preferences could be rightly decided. What a remarkable coincidence. At least Bork seems to envisage not voting judicially for some options which he would prefer as a legislator.

All this shows some of the dangers but also some of the excitement, involvement and intensity which the American confirmation process can unleash. I do not think that we are yet close to the day when a Select Committee of the House of Commons will have the right of veto over judicial nominees in the United Kingdom. But we do need to develop the infrastructure of analysis of potential judges. Whether or not we have the formal process, judges, future judges and those who appoint judges should know that we care about who is given the role of the judiciary in our democracy, that we have a vision of what that role entails and that we will criticize constructively and from an informed basis if judges do not meet those standards.

Towards Better Judging

——

I have shown, I hope, that the reality of judicial law-making lies somewhere between the Nightmare and the Noble Dream. I have endeavoured to present the judges as well-meaning individuals, admittedly from similar (but not identical) backgrounds, who disagree on their own role, on the pre-existing law in a dispute and on the most desirable way of developing the law in a particular area. I have tried to show how all this influences famous cases. I have not produced answers to profound questions but I have suggested where the prevailing theories themselves are inadequate. In particular, they tend to fasten on to one aspect of the truth rather than to paint the picture from all angles. Hence their tacit, and to my mind mistaken, assumption that there is only one right answer to the question of the proper role of judges in a democracy.

I do not intend to conclude by plucking general lessons from the preceding chapters. Instead, I have a confession to make, some criticisms to offer of the foregoing chapters in this book (in case the reader needs any encouragement in approaching this book critically) and some questions to ask as to what should happen next.

The confession is that I have the greatest respect for the contributions of Professors Dworkin and Griffith. I have emphasized my disagreements with them to add some spice to the debate. After all, they have the advantage of proposing a simple, superficially attractive thesis, which they can then refine (not to say, recant). That is one way in which to engage readers. Unfortunately, it is not necessarily the way to enhance our understanding but then those who steer a middle course might never persuade others to join the journey. By attacking them at the beginning of this book, I hope to have outraged their supporters and provoked them into reading this far. I am not going to retreat from anything which I have said but I do wish to record my appreciation of their views of the cathedral. So, whereas I began by highlighting what I take to be the hallucinogenic qualities in the fairy tale, the Noble Dream and the Nightmare, I would like to conclude by recording the flashes of reality amidst their fantasies.

First, the fairy tale still has its supporters. The entrance to Aladdin's cave is still guarded by some legal academics and practitioners, particularly some of those who specialize in common law and commercial matters. They feel that the modern vogue for 'law in context' has too much context and not enough law. They believe that there *are* rules which tell lawyers how to find the answers to present problems in past legal material. Precedent and statutory interpretation? That will do very nicely, sir. Are they living in a perpetual dream? No, for the most part the standard rules on precedent and statutory interpretation are very helpful. That is why most difficulties can be resolved by looking up the statutes or the cases without going anywhere near a court. And even when commercial cases come to court, there are powerful reasons why the judges should usually defer to the past law even if they think that a fairer solution could be achieved by some innovation. Commercial organizations on all sides of a problem will have been legally advised at all stages of the drafting of a contract, for example, and will have budgeted for the contract to be construed according to established legal techniques. In the international world of much modern business, it is also important to realize that the parties will often be able to choose a jurisdiction for arbitration or adjudication and will often choose the UK because of the reputation of its judges for keeping to tried and tested methods of interpretation.

But this area of the law is much different from the headline-grabbing world of Gillick, the GLC and GCHQ. In the areas of law with which we have been concerned, we are concerned precisely because the fairy tale can no longer guide us. That is why the cases go to the highest courts and are so often resolved by a split decision and a reversal of the lower courts. As I stressed in the first chapter, judicial law-making is not the be-all and end-all of a legal system. Judges and lawyers spend much more of their time applying settled law to unsettled facts. The importance of that work is obvious. But my focus has been something else, namely the contribution judges make to the development of the law in resolving hard cases. This is also important because it involves making new law, often overlapping with the work of Parliament and sometimes, according to some critics, usurping Parliament. That is one of the areas of judicial activity which rightly draws the attention of the media. There are others – the sentencing of criminals, for example, is something on which every leader-writer seems to have opinions. But I have chosen to concentrate on one area where the values of the law are thrown into sharp focus and where I feel that the real danger is the lack of understanding of what is really happening. This failure to see beyond the fairy tales exists both within the legal community and outside it among potential commentators. In trying to take these audiences beyond the fairy tale, I should not like to disillusion those who inhabit the Wonderland in which the magic passwords still work. That is simply another world.

If we leave fairyland behind, what should we do about dreamworld? What remains to be said about the Noble Dream? Is the Emperor really naked? No. Our initial misgivings at Dworkin's lack of familiarity with British law can now give way to respect for the way in which he weaves his cloak of integrity. He does not descend to British detail but he does tell a good story. We can apply the moral of his variation on the fairy tale to realistic settings for ourselves. His plot is admittedly transparent in that the ugly sisters of conventionalism and pragmatism are unable finally to suppress the beauty of Princess Integrity who lives happily ever after. But like the characters in fairy tales, Dworkin's inventions – goodies and baddies alike – are imprinted on our memories. Dworkin is painting the grand picture, creating the biggest soap opera of them all, his literally fantastic account purporting to explain legal life at a deeper level than the realistic description could ever hope to do. Dworkin's failure to wear British clothes leaves much work to be done. But *Law's Emperor* is not naked. Just as our children would be impoverished if nobody had made the effort to translate Hans Christian Andersen, so our legal system will be the poorer if tomorrow's British lawyers do not adapt Dworkin's noble dreams to the British stage.

That will require emphasizing the parts of his plot where he stresses the importance of moral discourse to legal argument, where he accepts that judges must address their constitutional role, and where he even begins to accept what he used to deny, that policy arguments are increasingly relevant to modern judicial decision-making.

So Dworkin is quite right, for example, to say that 'Lawyers are always philosophers, because jurisprudence is part of any lawyer's account of what the law is.' He is right to stress that 'law is an interpretive concept' and that judges engage in the task of interpretation not only when resolving hard cases but even when disposing of easy ones. I think he would agree with the spirit (although not the letter since he would supplement the idea of rules running out with his language of principles then running in) of a passage from my book on *Law and Morals* which has revisited me in bowdlerized form in many an examination script: 'the law student is not simply studying a morally neutral system of rules. When the rules are unclear or run out, as often happens in the topics covered at university, the moral nature of choices is often easier to discern. But even the settled rules have their roots in moral values . . . The law is not, cannot be, and should not be, morally neutral. But *which* moral values should it seek to enforce?' And Dworkin is right to make an important concession, even if he does seem to bury it in the foothills, or footnotes, of *Law's Empire*, namely that where a judge is interpreting a *statute*, then 'matters of policy are pertinent to his decision which rights the statute should be deemed to have created' (footnote 1 to chapter 9 of *Law's Empire*). Since statute law nowadays intrudes upon all manner of cases, there will be only a dwindling area of pure common law where 'policy' is ruled out for Dworkin.

Third, the Nightmare. I have argued that Griffith, the legal doyen of the Left, has in fact been invoked in a way which stifles a much-needed left-leaning critique of adjudication. It has become all too easy for Labour politicians to dismiss judges as conservative. But the message of this book is that law involves, above all, a commitment to *argument*, not simply to power. The Left has little power in Mrs Thatcher's Britain. The Government can win all the political disputes. But it does *not* win all the legal arguments. Of course, it begins with an advantage in that there is more Tory legislation on our statute books so that the judges are often, in local government cases for example, interpreting a statute which was explicitly designed to defeat the Left. Of course, the government can in theory conclude with an advantage by invoking parliamentary sovereignty to reverse a judicial decision through an Act of Parliament. But in between times, the judiciary do have the scope to call the government, and the rest of us, to account.

Griffith's book was first published in 1977 and is rooted in a different world where the roles were reversed. Labour had been in power since 1964 with only the interruption of the four-year Heath Government and seemed the natural party of government. The judges were then seen as an irritant *because* they called the politicians to account.

This see-sawing in political views of the judges is perhaps inevitable. It certainly has been a feature of American politics. Dworkin is equally firmly rooted in his formative years and context, still apparently trying to justify the liberal, activist Warren Court of the 1950s from the charge that it was 'undemocratic'. But another message of this book is that we must move with the times in our judging of judges. No single theory will suit all judiciaries in all places at all times for all sorts of cases. That is why the generalities of Dworkin are often nice but not determinative of particular hard cases. That is why Griffith's stirring critique has perhaps outlived its usefulness, why the Left now needs a more constructive approach to judicial decision-making.

But this should not blind us to the impact of Griffith's destructive thesis. Griffith was right to highlight several points about our judiciary. First, the judiciary is drawn from a narrow background. There ought to be more black judges, more female judges, judges from a wider net of schools and colleges. There will be. But I do not think that therefore condemns the present judiciary. And Griffith does not think that the new wave of judges will be much more liberal in their decisions because he seems to think that it is inherent in the judicial role to be conservative. Above all, what unites the present judiciary is their shared experience and socialization as barristers. But while I would like to see non-lawyers, philosopher-kings and queens, joining our most senior court, again I would not despair of barristers (indeed, Griffith is one). My ground for optimism is once more this commitment to argument, which is also part of lawyers' education.

But it was nevertheless Griffith's book which put the social composition of the judiciary on the media's agenda. He cannot be blamed for the way in which his text has sometimes been regarded as dogma beyond criticism. He can be praised for dramatically illustrating the importance of political consequences in judicial decision-making. He gave the lie to the fairy-tale account in which the past law is decisive, even if he took a one-sided view of how judges evaluated the policy arguments and even if he failed to offer a constructive account of the judicial role in our democracy.

If the fairy tale, the noble dream and the nightmare all have some merit, why is none of them completely realistic? At this point, we return to the image I conjured up at the beginning of this book. Each theorist is painting one view of the cathedral of law. If they are looking from the right or the left, or even from centre stage, there is a natural tendency to mistake the whole for the part. For a complete understanding of the cathedral, we need to walk around and reflect upon the many different images it provides. Above all, we need to get inside the cathedral to understand why it was built, what it is for, how it is used. Each picture adds something to our understanding of the cathedral and something to our understanding of the artist.

There is another point to bear in mind when assessing the impact of Dworkin and Griffith. Even those of us who are philistines when set against Dworkin's status as the doyen of legal culture vultures, know full well that perfectly accurate photographs of the cathedral at Rouen do not sell as well as would Monet's Impressionist studies. Dworkin and Griffith can capture the imagination through their bold-brush approach even if the picture looks a little blurred when contrasted with the real thing.

So we should place Dworkin and Griffith in perspective. So long as we do not elevate their occasional insights into dogma, there is considerable advantage in paying attention to their perspectives. But the danger is that we get diverted into theoretical defending and attacking of theses, while getting steadily further and further away from the practical reality of formulating a structure for legal argument so as to assist the judges in judging hard cases. Brian Barry has warned of this process in a perceptive review of Dworkin's collection of essays, *A Matter of Principle*:

> Let me describe the life-cycle of the typical Dworkinian controversy. In the first stage Dworkin announces some thesis which is unorthodox and striking. The second stage is marked by attacks on the thesis by critics who bring up all kinds of difficulties. Dworkin then replies to his critics and defends the thesis. Like a prudent sea-captain in a storm, however, he usually jettisons some of his cargo to save the rest. In the process of defending the thesis, terms are subtly redefined and claims modified so that at the end it loses in power what it has gained in plausibility. This is the third stage. Subsequent stages can be generated indefinitely by the iteration of the second and third stages. The theoretical limit of the sequence is constituted by a state of entropy in which the thesis, while undeniable, is no longer worth denying because it no longer says anything distinctive.

And I must say that I am not interested in playing such games, at least with Dworkin's work. But suppose people want to play games with this book? My thesis may not be as 'unorthodox and striking' as Dworkin's or Griffith's, nor as simple, but perhaps I should clarify what is my thesis, if only so that those who wish to progress beyond Barry's first stage can know what exactly to attack. My thesis is that judicial decisions are, and should be, influenced by many factors which can be usefully analysed under three main headings: first, the judges' view of the past law (statutes, precedents and principles); second, the judges' evaluation of the consequences of the options before them; third, the judges' view of their own role. I claim that these factors are not always acknowledged by judges, who often prefer to squeeze them into the first issue, but that they are always at work and that if judges were to be more candid, this would help the quality of their law-making. I insist, contrary to some commentators and some judges, that judges *are* entitled to take account of the consequences of their decisions. I insist, contrary to most commentators and some judges, that different views of the judicial role are legitimate, even within the same court at the same time. With more support, perhaps, I remind readers that the judicial roles will vary even more as we move from time to time, court to court, and topic to topic.

That is the positive side of the 'thesis'. My view that there is a legitimate diversity of judicial roles needs to be expanded. As an indication of what I mean, perhaps a brief explanation would help. Dworkin, Griffith and more or less everyone else who writes about judges share an unarticulated assumption, namely that there is only one right answer to the question of the role of judges in a democracy. Thus we hear that judges should defer to the legislature, or should defer to their predecessors, or should be more innovative and override past law, and so on.

But what we should be considering is whether talk of 'judges' in general is itself mistaken. Why should all judges share the same vision of their own role? We do not expect all legislators to do so. We expect different members of a sports team to pursue different roles within the common enterprise. It is only realistic to accept that judges *do* disagree on their proper role. I would go further and say that there *should* be a diversity of role perceptions.

Lord Denning, as we have seen, was an iconoclast. He was out of line with the normal approach of other judges. That poses problems for Dworkin, Griffith and co. But on my analysis Denning's individuality does not mean that he or other judges were mistaken. The system should tolerate the occasional maverick although it might break down if all the judges were so idiosyncratic.

In particular, it seems to me that judges' creativity ought to vary according to four factors:

1 Does the case involve statutes or common law (the latter allowing more freedom)?
2 Where is the judge in the courts' hierarchy (the higher up, the more creativity is suitable)?
3 Is the subject-matter such that certainty or justice is more important?
4 What is the likelihood of other institutions of government correcting any injustice?

Thus a first-instance judge in a commercial court should not allow his notions of justice to overtake his commitment to precedent.

He might be interpreting a statute, he is not an appellate judge, his area is one in which both parties will have been professionally advised and will have planned their businesses on the basis of the past law. But a Law Lord in the *Spycatcher* case should rightly regard himself as having much more freedom of action to do whatever he thinks is right.

More controversially, I believe that different Law Lords will legitimately differ on the degree of flexibility which they allow themselves. This is obviously what *does* happen on the United States' Supreme Court. And I, for one and perhaps only one, think that it *should* happen. Otherwise, I am not sure that we really need so many (nine on the Supreme Court) judges in our appellate courts. The clash between different interpretations of the judicial role in a democracy is exposed most starkly by the Supreme Court and its appointment procedures. But it is also true of British appeal courts. The line between proper and improper judicial roles is constantly in need of being redrawn as circumstances change (such as the comparative legitimacy and willingness of other branches of government to develop the law). It is therefore healthy to have competing views jostling for acceptance within the judiciary. The task of judging judges is a dynamic, not a static, one. Each generation will need to rewrite the rules of the game. But the rules allow a variety of tactics by which judges can score goals, although I should hasten to add that some moves should be ruled offside by the referees, who in this case are other judges, commentators and the public.

Judges are notoriously reluctant to admit the importance of conflicting conceptions of their own role. But their decision-making would benefit from such an admission. The thrust of this book has been that the past law is not the only decisive factor in an appellate judicial decision. Nevertheless, it is a significant consideration. Moreover, once we admit that other influences come into play, we can hope for greater candour about what the past law actually says instead of pretending that it says what we want it to say. The present tendency to collapse all questions into an analysis of the past law distorts that past legal material. Separating questions of consequences and roles should clarify the task of interpreting the old law.

The negative side of my thesis is that I disagree with anyone who maintains that judicial decisions should ignore 'policy', if by policy they mean consequences and the values by which we declare the consequences desirable or disastrous, and that I disagree with those who say that the whole truth, or even very much of the truth, can be discerned by looking at the judges' background.

It may be, of course, that we should not identify Dworkin with the former, or Griffith with the latter, view. Indeed, I would be the first to thank them for the insights which they do offer. In particular, I think both are acutely aware of the need to locate judicial resolution of hard cases within a theory of democracy, the Constitution and politics. Dworkin is most notably aware of the need also to root our speculations on the judiciary within a philosophical framework. Griffith is especially aware of the need to relate what we say about hard cases with the cases themselves. In any individual case, of course, Griffith and Dworkin might well agree with each other, and with me, on how the judges should have resolved the matter. It is my belief that we will be better able to pinpoint the reasons why we disagree in other cases, if we follow something like the framework which I have offered.

But it is only a framework, which leaves readers with the task of developing what Barry might call the second stage of criticizing and building on what I have written. I make no apologies for the limited utility of my conclusions. Even academics who are twice my age, such as Griffith and Dworkin, have not been able to apply all their experience so as to provide a comprehensive answer to all the questions surrounding judicial law-making in a democracy. Indeed, it is my contention that nobody can do that once and for all. I repeat my view that each generation must rethink the answers since the judicial role will surely rise and fall as the other institutions of government gain or lose legitimacy and the ability to use their authority for the development of the law. It is, at least, a start if we can agree on the right questions to ask and it is this, modest, task which I have attempted.

How should critics proceed in their efforts to develop answers? I think that the first factor, judicial views of the past law, has been analysed *ad nauseam*. More profitable areas for reflection are the other two kinds of influences. In particular, much work remains to be done on breaking down my general category of 'consequences' by determining which kinds of consequences are legitimate ones for the judges to take into account. I have left this vague up until now, partly because I do not know the answers but mostly because readers, especially students, can now reread the examples looking more closely for points which might have eluded them. Of course, many readers will already have spotted the different types of consequences which have been invoked, without being told to look for them. For example, in *Duport Steels v. Sirs*, the Law Lords were concerned not only with the consequences in the instant strike and in industrial relations generally, but they were mostly worried by the consequences for the judiciary themselves. They did not like what the steelworkers were doing in the immediate dispute, but the long-term consequences for industrial relations were minimal since Parliament was going to change the statutory law anyway in the near future. But the Law Lords were very sensitive about the way in which the Court of Appeal's decision reflected on the judges, and made this quite clear in their judgments which called for restraint so as to preserve the long-term power of the judges. The consequences at stake, therefore, were not only those for the litigants in the case. They would be the primary group to have in mind. But there are secondary, tertiary and even more indirectly affected groups to consider.

The question of the proper role of the judges also needs clarification. I have suggested that most commentators have an unarticulated assumption that there is one right role. If that were true, or course, many judges ought to change their practice. It is clear that judges on the Supreme Court have not only differed in their substantive values but also in their approach to their role. I see nothing wrong or surprising in this. Nor am I worried by the occasional iconoclast, like Lord Denning, within the British legal system. Lord Denning was not 'wrong' to be more adventurous than his colleagues, to be more interested in the consequences than in the precedents. The great judge will stand out from the crowd because he does perceive his role in a different way, because he challenges the received wisdom on the limits of the judicial role.

I have not begun to answer these questions. The balance

between the judges following the past law and changing it to suit their vision of the future needs at least another book on constitutional theory (again, watch this space). Our understanding of judges needs much more quantitative analysis of their voting patterns. There is much to be done.

I believe that the framework of analysis set out in this book is one small step in the right direction towards judging judges justly. But I leave the reader with the hope that we will soon take some giant leaps forward in the judging of judges. This book may have encouraged readers, perhaps even judges, to consider some of the following proposals:

1 Why don't appellate judges agree to consider explicitly the three factors of past law, future consequences and their constitutional role, ideally adopting a common format to their judgments, viz. dividing them into: the facts, the legal statutes, precedents and principles; the likely consequences and the desirability or otherwise thereof; the role of the judge; the reasons for disagreeing with colleagues or judges below; and finally, the decision?

2 Why doesn't Parliament pass a statute which acknowledges and encourages the occasional practice of the Law Lords to call the attention of the Law Commission or Parliament to any unsatisfactory element within the law which has been thrown up by litigation but which the judges feel unable to change themselves, and why doesn't Parliament promise to debate, and where necessary act upon, such issues within a reasonable time span?

3 Why don't judges recognize their role as law-makers as well as dispute-settlers by making more use of their inherent power to call for *amici curiae* to assist their judicial law-making by putting arguments which transcend the interests of the parties to the litigation?

4 Why don't counsel make more use of the American-style 'Brandeis briefs' which present detailed economic and social information to the judges so as to provide them with the facts on which to base their conclusions as to the consequences of their decisions?

5 Why don't senior judges employ law clerks, research assis-

tants, legal secretaries or *referendaires* to prepare the ground-work for their task of law-making?

6 Why isn't there radio and television coverage of the appellate courts, at least the House of Lords, again in recognition of the fact that, like Parliament, the judges are engaged in developing the law?

7 Why don't the Law Lords call press conferences when issuing their judgments in cases of great public interest instead of allowing their reasons to be lost in a welter of ill-informed criticism?

8 Why don't we have non-lawyers appointed straight to the Judicial Committee of the House of Lords in acknowledge-ment of the fact that the Law Lords are not just deciding technical questions of law but are facing the same kinds of issues which are examined, for example, by the philosopher-kings and queens who chair government committees of inquiry?

9 Why don't our legislators, journalists and academic lawyers take a more active interest in who is being appointed to the courts, developing the kind of infrastructure which helps the USA judge its judges, even if we choose not to follow their example of a formal procedure for such scrutiny?

10 Above all, how can we open up the dialogue between the judges and the judged which is at the heart of a democracy?

I would like readers to ponder and act upon these questions. If I can just point towards an answer to the last question, I hope that the media will devote an increasing amount of time, space and intelligence to the task of covering the law-making activities of the judges. The media are the transmission belt by which the public gets to hear of judicial decisions and by which the judges get to hear of popular reaction. This book is an attempt to provide some of the depth which cannot be covered in any one journalistic reaction to any one judicial decision. It has been written in the belief that the best constraint on the 'unelective dictatorship' is an informed public and, more positively, that the best aid to good judicial law-making is a judiciary which is informed as to public opinion on its role and the consequences of its decisions. The judges must not slavishly follow popular prejudice, of course, and the public must not expect such docility. What each is entitled to expect is the willingness to listen to each other and to be candid in what is influencing judicial law-making. I hope that this book has advanced the cause of such a dialogue between the judges and the judged.

Postscript

——

Judging Judges on Appeal

———

The scene is Hampstead where London's legal glitterati are indulging in their favourite pastime, cocktail-party jurisprudence. The characters are fictitious, like their reviews. To emphasize that this is fiction, the leading lawyers are cast as black women since there are, as yet, no black female QCs or judges in our real world.

Enter Roberta Lightweight QC. She looks in the mirror, takes a glass of wine and says to the first important person she can find:

'Darling, how wonderful to see you. I say, I saw something the other day which might interest you – a book called *Judging Judges*. Outrageous attempt to undermine the Bill of Rights idea and a bit rude about Ronnie and John . . .'

'Oh I know,' responds Mrs Justice Leonora Haughty. 'I was *so* annoyed that some whippersnapper should be so disrespectful – to Ronnie especially. How anyone could criticize *Law's Empire*, I shall never know. I thought it was just wonderful. Did you know that I read it on my cycling holiday in France last summer?'

Leonora is an old friend, formerly a semi-academic lawyer, who still likes to think of herself as a legal philosopher. If we are looking for a candidate to play the part of the old Minister, she is our woman. You will recall that the old Minister is sent by Hans Christian Andersen's Emperor to inspect the work in progress and is troubled to find no substance. Scared that he will be thought foolish, however, the old Minister proclaims loudly that it is a wonderful cloak, only to be embarrassed by the little boy who sees that the Emperor is naked. Leonora is worried that she has been found out. She has been boring everybody for months with the story of how she has read *Law's Empire* and thought it brilliant. If somebody is doubting this, then Leonora's dignity is at stake. She thinks (mistakenly) that *Judging Judges* is an unremitting assault on Dworkin. This calls for a stout defence of *Law's Empire*. She unjustly judges *Judging Judges*. She appoints herself the Supreme Arbiter of legal thought. She becomes Law's Umpire. She begins to ramble through a series of half-baked notions about what she does as a judge:

'I mean, Ronnie's absolutely right that my job is to search for the one right answer inherent in the existing law. Of course, John Griffith has a point in saying that some of my colleagues get the wrong end of the stick because they have a narrow outlook. But by and large we rise above our background and find the right principle. These ivory tower academics who have the cheek to tell us what we do just don't know what goes on in court. They are always looking for some hidden explanation when the deeper truth is staring them in the face – thank goodness that Ronnie has stood up for the traditional view that judges only declare the law.'

This conflates most of the possible theories of adjudication. There are hints of the fairy tale, the nightmare and the noble dream. Perhaps Leonora has become too dependent on teams of lawyers clarifying arguments for her. On her own, she is confused. Still, she is supported by Roberta's sycophancy:

'Oh, I couldn't agree more. I was livid when I read that chapter on the Bill of Rights. The man doesn't seem to understand what we've gone through to get the public to accept lawyers – scarcely a year has gone by without me signing something or other – you know, the Gang of 100 SDP supporters, Charter 88 and the rest. Then we get a lawyer, of all people, trying to undermine the whole thing. These academics just don't understand politics.'

A young well-informed BBC producer, Siobhan, joins the lawyers and asks about the questions raised by *Judging Judges* for media coverage of the law. This drives a wedge between Roberta and Leonora. Roberta fancies seeing herself on television. Leonora also fancies seeing herself on television but feels a responsibility to protect her colleagues from the rough and tumble of media treatment. Leonora responds first:

'Well, I've never seen such a silly idea as the proposal to have press conferences after cases.'

'Why is that silly?'

'Well, it just is. I suppose the idea is to probe us for our "real" reasons, to try to make out that we have made our decision because we went to a certain kind of school or university. It undermines the dignity of the law. We're not politicians, you know.'

'It undermines the dignity of a judge if she misrepresents an author. You know full well that Lee asks about press conferences in cases of great public interest precisely to make sure that the judges' printed reasons are covered by the media. He's thinking of *Spycatcher*, if you've read that chapter, and the way in which the media fastened on the dissents, ignoring the majority's explanations. Surely it's got to be a good idea to think about communicating reasons in such a way that they will be understood by the public. He doesn't mean a press conference like the ones Bobby Robson has to suffer after a disappointing England soccer game. He means Joshua Rozenburg or some other reliable legal journalist asking the presiding judge to explain, in a nutshell, why the decision was reached.'

'I don't write my judgments for the *Nine O'Clock News*, you know.'

'Who do you write them for?'

'The litigants, their lawyers, future lawyers.'

'And the public doesn't matter?'

'Of course the public matters but they can read it in *The Times* Law Report.'

'But people take their news from television nowadays and even if we stick to newspapers, the widely-read papers don't have a law report. Doesn't the majority of the public count?'

'What do you think?'

'I think that politicians take care to have press conferences to explain their proposals for law reform. They want to reach the whole public.'

'But they have to do that because they are elected.'

'All the more reason for the unelected judges to be properly understood, so that they can be accountable through public scrutiny and criticism to the public they are meant to serve. Anyway, I think the question about press conferences is a good one because it makes you think about the differences between law-making by politicians and by judges. But there's another aspect to media involvement: what about televising key appeals?

Why can we film the Lords in their legislative capacity but not when they act judicially? And why can Channel 4 run a version of a court case with actors reading transcripts but not show the real thing?'

Roberta steps in, much to the relief of Leonora who was just about to say that if Siobhan is a typical example of media interviewers then she has no intention of submitting herself to a press conference. Roberta supports television cameras in court and gives Siobhan her telephone number in case she wants an expert view on any television programme about law or anything else. Roberta didn't get where she is today by being bashful about her own abilities. Neither did Leonora, come to think of it. Anyway, we rejoin the party later, by which time the conversation has returned, via a tedious account of their day in court, to the issue of what judges are doing in hard cases. Siobhan asks innocently:

'Did I hear you say something about judges only declaring the law?'

'Absolutely,' beams Leonora.

'But surely since the 1966 Practice Statement, it is obvious that judges *do* make law in at least those cases where the Law Lords overrule their own previous decisions?'

'Well, in a rather trivial sense, yes, but only where there has been a mistake somewhere along the line. The Law Lords are still drawing out the underlying Dworkinian principles.'

'OK but what were the judges doing in the earlier case, then?'

'Look, nobody is suggesting that we are always right, nor that we always agree, just that we are always looking for something which is latent in the law.'

'That's what you may think you are doing but why do we have to accept your interpretation of your task? Aren't you really finding something latent in your own psyche, as Griffith might argue?'

'I would be the first to admit that Griffith has a point. In practice we may be flawed but in principle our task is clear – only Parliament has the right to change the law's direction, our role is to keep the law heading in the same direction.'

'But you're shifting ground all the time, running through the different theories of adjudication – mixing a Dworkin-and-

Griffith cocktail with what now seems like a dash of Devlin. Doesn't that show that *Judging Judges* is right to take a walk around the cathedral of law before suggesting the need for a variety of vantage points?'

'No, because Lee's implication is still that we can do what we like, taking account of what we like.'

'No, Lee's point is that any so-called "principles of integrity" are complex value judgements based on an intuitive assessment not only of the past but also of the future and your role as the transmission belt between the two. You will be affected by your evaluation of the consequences of your decision, or in Dworkin-speak you will be trying to find the principle which best fits and justifies the law. It's better in those circumstances to be open about it and to receive explicit argument about the consequences of alternative courses of action, otherwise we get law-making by default. Of course, there's a further disagreement as to whether there can be any such thing as one coherent, seamless web of integrity running through the law, as you seem to think, or whether the law is a bundle of tensions between competing values.'

'Look, if you are prepared to argue with me about the merits of any particular decision, that shows that you are accepting the truth that there is an answer lurking underneath the existing law. When you criticize my judgments, you are implicitly acknowledging the one-right-answer thesis because that's the standard by which you are judging my judgment.'

'Not at all. I am implicitly accepting the opposite – that there are many ways of interpreting any text, legal, theological or literary. There is no single right answer which can be "found" independently of the interpreter. That's one of the insights I take for granted in this post-structuralist, CLS world.'

Leonora nearly chokes. This is unfair. Her interrogator is using long words and initials in an attempt to unsettle her. She looks to Roberta who has already looked away like an ill-prepared student dodging the tutor's eye. Siobhan tries to make it simple for Leonora and Roberta.

'Look, I don't know much about Critical Legal Studies myself and I don't particularly want to get into all that dungarees-and-deconstructionism but the simplest way of putting it is to think about literary theory. After all, Mrs Justice Haughty, I've always thought of you as the Morris Zapp of the Small Legal World.'

Leonora is still lost. She packs Dworkin's book in her holiday knapsack, remember. She prefers allusions to Shakespeare rather than to twentieth-century literature. Indeed, while she's thinking about it, that's one of the things she most liked about *Law's Empire*. On the other hand, Roberta knows what's going on – she may not have read anything for which she wasn't paid since she became a barrister but she does watch television. She's seen the television adaptation of David Lodge's book, *Small World*.

'Now, just remind me, Zapp is . . . ?'

'You know, you must remember his lecture – "every decoding is another encoding . . . The attempt to peer into the very core of a text, to possess once and for all its meaning, is vain – it is only ourselves that we find there, not the work itself. Freud said . . ." '

'Yes, I know what Freud said, thank you very much,' interjects Leonora, who hasn't got a clue what Freud said but who makes a mental note to catch up on some jurisprudence. It sounded as if jurisprudence was now much more interesting than when she had taught it (or perhaps it was the way she had taught it).

Roberta realizes when she is out of her depth which, jurisprudentially speaking, is whenever you let go of the edge of the shallow end. She brings the conversation back to her third love – after herself and the law – middle-ground politics:

'But bringing the whole debate back to basics, the trouble with *Judging Judges* is that it is lukewarm about a Bill of Rights.'

Siobhan responds: 'But is it? Isn't it saying that we should beware the leaders of a revolution – what do they have to gain? When the proponents of constitutional reform turn out to be social democrat lawyers, aren't we entitled to ask why we should trust lawyers rather than those politicians who are voted in by the electorate? *Judging Judges* is drawing attention to the fact that the interpreters of a Bill of Rights will have great power and that we ought, therefore, to expect great attention paid to the detail of their selection and monitoring before we formalize the transition of power to the judges. It's not hostility to the Bill of Rights so much as a warning that it's not a panacea and that the debate about it should be the occasion for extracting a more accountable system of selecting judges. Surely you can't disagree with that?'

Roberta comes perilously close to making a good point: 'Well, of course I want the best judges to be appointed [all three know how to decode that message – viz. Roberta is desperate to become a judge herself] but I am a little bit worried about the idea of monitoring judges, as the chapter on Bork shows [all three know how to decode that as well – viz. Roberta does not want to be on the receiving end of the kind of cross-examination she loves to conduct]. The greatest danger [and here comes the semi-good point] is that judges and proto-judges will be looking over their shoulder to the verdict of some committee rather than focussing on the justice of the case.'

'Of course, that is a danger but surely it all depends on how it is done. Anyway, potential judges are monitored already through gossip and hear-say. Again, *Judging Judges* is just asking for a more systematic, open, accountable, comprehensive monitoring. I can understand that judges would be reluctant to be labelled conservative or liberal. I can see that judging isn't like that – in fact *Judging Judges* stresses that, doesn't it? Judges can't be typecast in that way. So-called "liberals" can be tough on sentencing and "conservatives" can be soft. Some are tougher on crimes of violence, others on "striped-collar crime" like insider dealing. Hard-nosed commercial cases can't be divided into conservative and liberal views. But the monitoring could be much more sophisticated than simply labelling judgments right wing or left wing . . .'

Leonora interrupts Siobhan to ask how she knows so much about law in general and the judging of judges in particular.

'I studied law at university. I read the book because I'm in current affairs.'

'And have you read the other books criticized in *Judging Judges*?'

'Yes, of course . . .'

Roberta is indeed way, way out of her depth. She has seen *reviews*, needless to say, of *The Politics of the Judiciary*, *Law's Empire* and now *Judging Judges*. Leonora has read *Law's Empire*, skimmed the other two and understood none of them. Things have come to a pretty pass when a reading of the reviews, or a flicking through the index to see if one is mentioned, are insufficient for holding one's own in a discussion about law with a journalist.

Siobhan continues: '. . . After all, you lawyers are always telling us journalists to learn some law before we try to report on your profession. And the basic principles of the two professions are the same, aren't they? Brief yourself properly before you talk about something. Keep up to date, don't rely on what you learnt at school. Be fair. Get a variety of viewpoints before you choose the best angle for a story. And, above all, as we are doing and as *Judging Judges* recommends, talk it through, argue about it and think about it. Don't just cling to orthodoxy because it's comfortable. Don't just rely on other people's views. Think for yourself.'

With that, Siobhan brings the conversation to a close. Roberta has been staring past Siobhan throughout the discussion, looking at herself in the mirror and half-wondering about the painting she can see, somewhat distorted, in the reflection. Siobhan turns Roberta round 180 degrees, points to the picture on the far wall and says with reference to the Monet print:

'You will get a much clearer picture of the Cathedral at Rouen from this perspective.'

Quoting Morris Zapp's explanation as to why those who are cynical about one-right-answer theses still indulge in argument, Siobhan leads Roberta and Leonora towards their hostess:

' "We maintain our position in society by publicly performing a certain ritual, just like any other group of workers in the realm of discourse – lawyers, politicians, journalists. And as it looks as if we have done our duty for today, shall we all adjourn for a drink?" '

Notes, Suggestions for Further Reading and Acknowledgements

NB Where I give the references to cases, I have first given the official law reports and then the *All England Law Reports*. Law students will have access to the former in their libraries and will know the abbreviations (eg, AC = Appeal Cases). If possible, they should read the cases in the official reports because these begin with counsels' arguments which are so important for understanding the direction which a judgment takes but which are so often ignored by commentators who blame or praise the judges when the real heroes or villains are the lawyers who argue before them. 'General readers' who are really determined to read a judgment in full can usually track down the *All England Law Reports*, published by Butterworths, in a major public library. *The Times*, the *Independent*, the *Guardian* and the *Financial Times* perform a valuable service in publishing abridged reports of important cases but it is obviously better to read the full version wherever possible.

Chapter 1

Lord Reid, 'The Judge as Law-Maker' 12 *Journal of the Society of Public Teachers of Law* 22 (1972)

Professor Hart, 'American Jurisprudence through English Eyes: The Nightmare and the Noble Dream' in Hart, *Essays in Jurisprudence and Philosophy* (OUP, 1983) Ch. 4

R. Dworkin, *Taking Rights Seriously* (Duckworth, revised ed, 1978)
— *A Matter of Principle* (OUP, 1986)
— *Law's Empire* (Fontana, 1986)

J. Griffith, *The Politics of the Judiciary* (Fontana, 3rd ed, 1985)

G. Calabresi and D. Melamed, 'Property Rules, Liability Rules, and Inalienability: One View of the Cathedral' (1972) 85 *Harvard Law Review*

I. Kennedy and S. Lee, 'This rush to judgment', *The Times*, 1 April 1987

S. Lee, *'Spycatcher'*, *The Times*, 14 August 1987

H. L. A. Hart, 'Immorality and Treason', *Listener*, 30 July 1959

See Dworkin, *A Matter of Principle* for several essays which first appeared in the *New York Review of Books*

S. Lee, *Law and Morals* (OUP, 1986)

Chapter 2

K. Minogue, 'The Biases of the Bench', *Times Literary Supplement*, 6 January 1978

R. Cross, *Statutory Interpretation* (second edition by J. Bell and G. Engle, Butterworths, 1987)

L. Goldstein [ed.], *Precedent in Law* (OUP, 1988)

J. Raz, *The Authority of Law* (OUP, 1980) Ch. 10

Lord McCluskey, *Law, Justice and Democracy* (Sweet & Maxwell, 1987)

Chapter 3

A. Hutchinson, 'Indiana Dworkin and Law's Empire' (1987) 96 *Yale Law Journal* 637

AG v. Jonathan Cape [1976] QB 752, [1975] 3 All ER 484

McLoughlin v. O'Brian [1983] AC 410, [1982] 2 All ER 298

Sidaway v. Royal Bethlem Hospital Governors [1985] AC 871, [1985] 1 All ER 643

Chapter 4

Hatton case = *R. v. Liverpool City Council, ex p. Ferguson, The Times*, 20 November 1985

Labour Research, January 1987

Lord Wedderburn, *The Worker and the Law* (3rd ed, Penguin, 1986)

I. Kennedy, 'A Reply to the Politics of the Judiciary' (1983–4) 33 King's Council 9

Chapter 5

Secretary of State v. Tameside [1977] AC 1014, [1976] 3 All ER 665
TSB case = *Ross v. Lord Advocate*
Spycatcher case = *Attorney General v. Guardian Newspapers*
R v. Secretary of State for the Environment, ex p. Ostler [1977] QB 122 [1976] 3 All ER 90
Brown v. Board of Education (1954) 347 US 483

Chapter 6

R v. Lemon [1979] AC 617, [1979] 1 All ER 898

Chapter 7

Duport Steels v. Sirs [1980] 1 WLR 142 [1980] 1 All ER 529

Chapter 8

Bromley v. GLC [1983] 1 AC 768 [1982] All ER 129

Chapter 9

Mandla v. Lee [1983] QB 1 (CA); [1983] 2 AC 548 (HL); [1982] 3 All ER 1108 (CA); [1983] 1 All ER 1062 (HL)
Wheeler v. Leicester [1985] AC 1054, [1985] 2 All ER 151

Chapter 10

Council of Civil Service Unions v. Minister for the Civil Service [1985] AC 374, [1984] 3 All ER 935

Chapter 11

Gillick v. DHSS [1986] AC 112, [1985] 3 All ER 402

Chapter 12

Thomas v. NUM (South Wales Area) [1986] Ch 20, [1985] 2
  All ER 1

Chapter 13

Ross v. Lord Advocate [1986] 1 WLR 1078 [1986] 3 All ER 79

Chapter 14

C v. S [1987] 2 WLR 1108 [1988] 1 All ER 1230
Re B (a minor) [1988] AC 199 [1987] 2 All ER 206

Chapter 15

Attorney General v. Guardian Newspapers [1987] 3 All ER 316

Chapter 16

H. J. Abraham, *Justices and Presidents* (2nd ed. OUP, 1985) to
  which I am indebted for the American league tables.
G. Lewis, *Lord Atkin* (Butterworths, 1983)
R. Heuston, *The Lives of the Lord Chancellors 1940–70*
  (OUP, 1987)
A. Paterson, *The Law Lords* (Macmillan, 1982)
C. Harlow, *Public Law and Politics* (Sweet & Maxwell, 1986),
  Ch. 10

Chapter 17

Lord Denning, *The Discipline of Law* (Butterworths, 1979)
  — *The Due Process of Law* (Butterworths, 1980)
  — *The Family Story* (Butterworths, 1981)
  — *What Next in the Law* (Butterworths, 1982)
  — *The Closing Chapter* (Butterworths, 1983)
  — *Landmarks in the Law* (Butterworths, 1984)
J. Jowell and P. McAuslan, *Lord Denning* (Sweet & Maxwell,
  1984)

Chapter 18

Lord Devlin, *The Judge* (OUP, 1979)
— 'Judges, Governments and Politics' (1978) MLR 501
— *Easing the Passing* (Faber, 1986)
— *The Enforcement of Morals* (OUP, 1965)
H. L. A. Hart, *Law, Liberty and Morality* (OUP, 1964)

Chapter 19

Lord Hailsham, *The Door Wherein I Went* (Collins, 1975)
R v. Howe [1987] AC 417 [1987] 1 All ER 771

Chapter 20

Lord Scarman, *English Law – the New Dimension* (Sweet & Maxwell, 1974)

Chapter 21

Lord Mackay, Maccabaean Lecture, delivered at the British Academy, 2 December 1987.

Chapter 22

M. Zander, *A Bill of Rights?* (3rd ed, Sweet & Maxwell, 1985)
A. Lester, 'The United Kingdom Isolated' (1984) *Public Law*
Lord McCluskey, *Law, Justice and Democracy* (Sweet & Maxwell, 1987)
Roe v. Wade (1973) 410 US 113
Bowers, Attorney General of Georgia v. Hardwick (1986) 106 S.Ct. 2841
Goldman v. Weinberger (1985) 106 S.Ct. 1310
H. Abraham, *Justices and Presidents* (Oxford University Press, 2nd ed, 1985)
Sunday Times v. UK (1979) 2 EHRR 245
Rees v. UK (1987) 9 EHRR 56
Johnston v. Ireland (1987) 9 EHRR 203
GCHQ – see chapter 10

Judge Learned Hand, *The Spirit of Liberty* (New York, 1959)
G. Gilmore, *The Ages of American Law* (Yale, 1978)

Chapter 23

The Bork controversy can most easily be studied through the excellent collection of materials in the *Cardozo Law Review* special issue of October 1987 (volume 9).

Dworkin's three articles on Bork can be found in the *New York Review of Books* issues of 8 November 1984, 13 August 1987 and 17 December 1987.

For Bork's own views on the theories of adjudication, see 'Neutral Principles and Some first Amendment Problems' 47 *Indiana Law Journal 1* (1971) and 'The Constitution, Original Intent, and Economic Rights' 23 *San Diego Law Review* 823 (1986).

Chapter 24

B. Barry, *Times Literary Supplement*, 25 October 1985, 1195
D. Pannick, *Judges* (OUP, 1987)
M. Dockray, 'Television in the Courts', *1988 Modern Law Review*
R. Abel, *The Legal Profession in England and Wales* (Blackwell, 1988)

I have drawn on my earlier writing in diverse publications: *University of Pittsburgh Law Review*, *Oxford Journal of Legal Studies*, *Law Quarterly Review*, *Law and Justice*, *Oxford Essays in Jurisprudence*, *King's Counsel*, *Public Law*, *The Times*, the *Law Magazine*, the *Listener*. I am grateful to the editors and publishers for permission to do so. May I return the compliment by urging readers to follow legal developments in these and similar journals. I am particularly grateful to Ian Kennedy, with whom I wrote on the sterilization case as it was proceeding through the courts, and to Simon Whittaker, with whom I wrote a note in the *Law Quarterly Review* on the miners' strike, for permission to adapt and use here a few paragraphs which first appeared under our joint names. They should not be held responsible for the interpretation of these cases which I now offer.

I hope that readers will be encouraged to read what Dworkin, Griffith and others have to say for themselves:
R. Dworkin, *Taking Rights Seriously* (Duckworth, revised ed. 1978)
— *A Matter of Principle* (OUP, 1986)
— *Law's Empire* (Fontana, 1986)
J. Griffith, *The Politics of the Judiciary* (Fontana, 3rd edition 1985)
— 'The Political Constitution' (1979) 42 *Modern Law Review* 1

An invaluable analysis of contrasting views is:
J. Bell, *Policy Arguments in Judicial Decisions* (OUP, 1983). The best jurisprudential analysis along the lines I have been advocating is N. MacCormick, *Legal Reasoning and Legal Theory* (OUP, 1978), especially Ch 6. For those with access to a good law library, another valuable article is: P. Atiyah 'Judges and Policy' (1980) 15 *Israel Law Review* 346.

Finally, we all have free access to the courts. Please make a point of going to the Royal Courts of Justice in the Strand and the Judicial Committee of the House of Lords in the Palace of Westminster to hear and see legal argument for yourself. The appellate courts are worth visiting. You will see that the Law Lords at Westminster do not wear wigs and gowns. You will hear very sharp and relatively informal exchanges between the judges and counsel. If you cannot go to the law courts (and if you all did at the same time there would be chaos since there is seating only for about two dozen in the committee rooms at the Lords), then I believe that the appellate courts should come to you through the media of television and radio. One way or another, the aim of this book has been to encourage you to judge judges for yourself.

Here is the code which relates my short-hand terms for the cases with their full titles and which gives the dates of decisions:

Gay News = *R v. Lemon*, 21 February 1979

Steel Strike = *Duport Steels v. Sirs*, 7 February 1980

GLC = *Bromley v. GLC*, 17 December 1981

Discrimination = *Mandla v. Lee*, 24 March 1983, and *Wheeler v. Leicester City Council*, 25 July 1985

GCHQ = *Council of Civil Service Unions v. Minister for the Civil Service*, 22 November 1984

Gillick = *Gillick v. DHSS*, 17 October 1985

Miners' Strike = *Thomas v. NUM (South Wales Area)*, 11 February 1985

TSB = *Ross v. Lord Advocate*, 31 July 1986

Abortion = *C v. S*, 24 February 1987

Sterilization = *Re B (a minor) (sterilization)*, 30 April 1987

Spycatcher = *Attorney General v. Guardian Newspapers*, 30 July 1987

Index